Death of a Church Lady

Confessions of Hurt, Healing & Freedom

Teri Miller

Death of a Church Lady
Confessions of Hurt, Healing & Freedom
Copyright © 2017 by Teri Miller

Unless other wised noted all scripture are taken from the THE HOLY BIBLE, NEW INTERNATIONAL VERSION®, NIV® Copyright © 1973, 1978, 1984, 2011 by Biblica, Inc.® Used by permission. All rights reserved worldwide.

Scripture quotations taken from the Amplified® Bible (AMP), Copyright © 2015 by The Lockman Foundation Used by permission. www.Lockman.org

Scripture taken from The Message. Copyright © 1993, 1994, 1995, 1996, 2000, 2001, 2002. Used by permission of NavPress Publishing Group.

Scripture quotations marked (NLT) are taken from the Holy Bible, New Living Translation, copyright © 1996, 2004, 2007, 2013, 2015 by Tyndale House Foundation. Used by permission of Tyndale House Publishers, Inc., Carol Stream, Illinois 60188. All rights reserved.

ISBN: 978-0-692-94789-0
Library of Congress Control Number: 2017917019

Cover & Layout Design by Brandon & Jenna Day, ThinkTree Media
Author photograph by Carli Jeen, Carlijeen.com

Printed in the USA

To all of the teachers, preachers and friends
who have been used by God to speak truth to my
life: your influence has changed my perspective, my
thinking and ultimately my relationship with the
Lord. Your diligence is my reward.

To my amazing, generous, loving husband
I would not have written this book without your
encouragement and support. I'm still in love with
you and will be forever.

And to my amazing kids
who have encouraged me to write my story and have
inspired me to live my life honestly and without fear.

Table of Contents

Introduction

I confess, I am a church lady. I've been one all of my life. But this church lady had to die. Again. Galatians 2:20 says, *"I have been crucified with Christ; and it is no longer I who live, but Christ lives in me; and the life which I now live in the flesh I live by faith in the Son of God, who loved me and gave Himself up for me."* This scripture became reality in my life when I accepted Jesus as my Lord and Savior a long time ago. Little did I know then, the process of death and the revelation of truth would continue to be a reality throughout my whole life. Unfortunately, the journey with Christ isn't complete when we meet Him; that's only the beginning. For many of us, the journey gets clouded with religion, tradition, and striving. I know mine did. After serving God for over 40 years, He decided it was time to power wash my motives, thinking and understanding of who He is and who I am in Him.

I'm going to admit, right up front, that I've been hurt by the church. Devastated is more like it. I will give vague details regarding my experience in this book. However, and this is a big however, this book is not a tell-all or a rant on what is wrong with the church today. On the contrary, I still love to go to church. I still serve at church. I am still in relationship with the Church because I have been healed in my heart and set free in my thinking. Many people with a similar experience have not been. This is my primary motivation for writing this book. Many women, and men for that matter, are so wounded they can no longer continue to participate. Maybe that's you or someone you know. If it is, please hang in there with me. Don't let my journey go to waste. Don't let the fact that I still enjoy and attend my local church confuse you. The church lady is dead. The mask-wearing, judgment-toting, striving-to-belong church lady has gotten a much needed makeover. The chapters in this book will tell you how. It's amazing what God will do if you ask Him to reveal truth. I'm a different person then I was 5 years ago. Heck, I think differently and live differently than I did 6 months ago. I can't wait to see what He reveals to me tomorrow. What He has done for me, I know He will do for you.

THE ADJUSTMENT

Remember the phrase from the legendary hymn Amazing Grace, "I once was lost but now I'm found, was blind but now I see…" Well, this book isn't about the "once was lost" part. I was lost, but Jesus found me a long time ago, over 40 years ago. I prayed and asked Jesus to come into my life at age six during a Bible school class, and Psalm 71:5-6 expresses my heart well: *"For you have been my hope, O Sovereign Lord, my confidence since my youth. From birth I have relied on you; you brought me forth from my mother's womb. I will ever praise you."* I can associate with David because I feel like I've always known the Lord, but before you throw this book down because perhaps you can't relate to that scripture at all, trust me when I tell you that my life and journey are far from perfect. I have been serving the Lord and involved in church all of my life, but it may surprise you that I feel like I've just met Him. In many ways, I'm starting over. So why has it taken me so long to realize some fundamental truths? I'm not exactly sure, but I do know, the older I get and the longer I know the Lord, the more I realize how simple the truth of the gospel is. I was making it way too hard.

Which leads me to the "was blind, but now I see" part of the song. Lately, I don't see things like I used to. God is messing with my vision, my perspective, and I'm so glad. The past 40-something years have been great: full of answered prayers, provision of blessings and God's love in abundance, amazing times of worship with family and friends, and so much more. However, this book is my response to what I can only call a life-changing, freedom-delivering refocusing.

Let me put it this way, if you've ever been to the eye doctor, you know that they put this large apparatus (a phoropter) in front of you to look through. When your prescription is getting close to 20/20, you can see most of the bigger letters and some of the medium-sized ones too. The doctor makes a few more adjustments and turns the lenses a few more "clicks" and everything becomes clear. That's what I'm talking about! God has made adjustments to my thinking and perspective, and I am set free as a result.

"I had to get uncomfortable before I would be open."

These revelations are so basic to the Christian walk that I'm almost embarrassed to say it's taken me this long to get them. You may read this book and think "Girl… what's the matter with you? It's not that hard." I know that now, but as I talk with others about what God is doing in my life, I find that they too are discovering their true identity in Christ and are receiving new levels of His love and grace. I wish I could tell you that God's work in me is the result of a wonderful afternoon in my favorite quiet place, where the Lord miraculously downloaded His great truth and understanding to my life; but unfortunately, that was not the case. I had to get uncomfortable before I would be open. Life had to get messy before I would be totally willing. And I had to start looking up, if that makes any sense, before I could see what God was trying to show me. Regrettably, desperation, loneliness, and heartbreak were my ambassadors.

My story really isn't all that dramatic, but I'm telling it because perhaps God can use it to bring a new level of wisdom, revelation, healing and freedom to your life. That is my prayer. So grab a cup of coffee, take a seat in the "Doctor's" chair and see if the Great Physician wants to make a few adjustments. You may only need one "click," you may receive many, but if you're like me, you don't want to miss anything God has for your life.

1

Confession:
I Still Love Church

*"You are no longer foreigners and aliens, but fellow citizens
with God's people and members of God's household, built
on the foundation of the apostles and prophets, with Christ
Jesus himself as the chief cornerstone. In him the whole
building is joined together and rises to become a holy temple
in the Lord. And in him you too are being built together to
become a dwelling in which God lives by his Spirit."*
Ephesians 2:19-22

I still love church. I still love to go to church, but
then I always have. I love the people, the laughter
and hugs, the melody made by voices connecting
and the expectation of experiencing God's presence. For
most of my life, I have shown up early and been one
of the last people to leave. Just ask my kids. They will
confirm this. It's my kind of place, my kind of people.

Lately though, I've noticed there is a lot of talk about church. Talk about the way we "do" church, from the books I've read, sermons I've heard and conversations I have observed among my peers. It seems there is a wave of re-evaluation going on. People have been hurt. People are leaving the church and others are asking questions. Questions like: "Is church for the saved or the unsaved?", "Is the church effective in reaching and disciplining the lost?" and "Is what we are doing today what the Bible describes in the book of Acts?" Maybe I've noticed this trend because it's personally where I am. There are certain times in life when you pause to evaluate your priorities, and for me, the past five years have purified my ambitions, passions and priorities. Noticing this recent evaluation of church reminds me of when I got pregnant. Once I was lugging around my belly, I began to notice all of the other women who were pregnant too. I never noticed pregnant women before, but once it happened to me, I noticed every woman with that unmistakable belly. I also notice this phenomenon when I am shopping for a car. Once I start looking at a specific make and model, all of a sudden, the car I want is everywhere. Everyone else is driving "my" car. I guess my focus on how we do church and are we being the Church is similar to that.

From my observation, people, especially young people, are fed up with dead, dry church services. Religion is not meeting the needs in their lives, and they are looking for a genuine move of God. I guess that's why so many of them no longer feel the need to attend church. I absolutely understand this. Why go through the motions without receiving the reward of His love or presence? Sadly, many are not finding their way back to the house of God. This makes me sad. I am glad, however, that I'm not alone in my desire for God encounters in our meetings and in our lives that bring revelation, true identity and freedom. Who needs more religion in their life? No one.

I need to know the love of God that changes everything. I need power to live my life to the fullest. I need to forgive and to let go of the hurts that have occupied my heart for too long. I need to give my money, my time and my talents to the One who gave everything for me. How about you? If you are already there, say "Amen!" If not, let's press in together and get rid of bad thinking. Let's pursue truth together. It's time to live in freedom, and time for us to mature and walk in grace and love. I want to know Jesus. I want to know him more today than I did yesterday, and I want to know Him even more tomorrow. If it's not all about Him, then what are we doing? Being religious, I guess. That's why I still love to go to church after everything that's happened in my life (hang in there, we'll get there) the past several years. In church, it's all about Jesus. If it's not, you're in the wrong church.

EXPERIENCE BRINGS PERSPECTIVE

I grew up a church nomad, a spiritual mutt. As a child, my family usually went to church, but we never got planted anywhere. We were Baptist, Nazarene, charismatic ... and sometimes I even went to my friend's Catholic Church. I'm grateful for this upbringing now as I see it gave me such a well-rounded perspective on church and worship by experiencing so many styles, so many different ways to "do" church. Sometimes, though, it could get quite interesting, like the times when we would visit my aunt's church, a charismatic, very Spirit-led church, flowing in the gifts of the Spirit. I loved to visit her church because there was always so much to see. People would fall over after someone prayed for them. Others would be singing songs in languages I couldn't understand, but that didn't seem to matter, I always loved the sound. It was an interesting combination of curiosity, confusion (on my part) and peace. Then we would go back to the Baptist church we often attended, and it would be so different. The music was different, a Southern Baptist style, using four-part harmonies, great musicians, and dynamic presentation. I loved it there too. The pastor was an amazing man of God and a dynamic preacher. I can remember being afraid of him because he was tall and authoritative with a booming voice. Maybe I was afraid of him because of the times he came out into the congregation and walked on top of the pews to make a point or to tell some teenager to stop talking. However, even with his intimidating personality, I loved listening to him preach. Even as a child, he held my attention. I remember one time he slithered on the ground and took on the character of

Satan to make a point. That was powerful ... and a little scary to a 10-year-old. We visited many churches and that was ok because it gave us opportunity to experience how others worshiped God. I also enjoyed going to my best friend's Catholic Church. I enjoyed the formality of it all and how quiet it was, how different it was from what I was accustomed to. However, it used to bother me that when she was at church with me, she could take communion, but when I was at church with her, I had to wait in the pew while everyone else took communion. That used to bother me, but I'm over it now...really, I am. I think.

When I got into high school, we settled down at a Nazarene Church in our area. Several of my friends went there, and I enjoyed the youth group and began to sing in the choir. This was the first church that felt like home to me.

"For we are God's workmanship, created in Christ Jesus to do good works, which God prepared in advance for us to do."
Ephesians 2:10

FINALLY HOME

Looking back, I can see the relationship between serving and belonging. Up until this point, I never felt like any of the churches I attended were "my" church. As long as I walked in, received and walked out, I always felt like a visitor. When I began to know and be known by people, the whole dynamic changed for me. I was hooked. A young, teenage church lady was born.

If you are available and the Holy Spirit lives in you, and if you can love people, God will use you.

So, let me ask you a question. Do you feel like a visitor at your church? Do you see people laughing and interacting with each other and wonder how they do it? How do they know people so well? Let me tell you a secret I've learned: they are involved and they serve somewhere. They meet on Thursday mornings to study the Bible or fold the bulletins; they volunteer as an usher; they work in the nursery or sing in the choir, or maybe they just got back from a mission trip with others from the church, etc.

So let me ask you, do you serve at your church? If not, what is stopping you? Have you asked God what would be a good fit for you? I've heard my pastor ask, "What are you passionate about? What are you good at?" Sometimes it's that easy. It's a great place to begin if you are wanting to get involved and don't know where to start. Don't sweat it. God will get you where He needs you to be, either for your benefit or the benefit of others. (Usually, it's not either/or, because I'm always blessed when I serve.) The hard part is taking the first step. You may not feel qualified. Fantastic! You're probably not. Now you will have to rely on God to help you, and you will be desperate for Him to move through you. Zechariah 4:6 says, *"Not by might nor by power, but by my Spirit, says the Lord Almighty."* If you are available and the Holy Spirit lives in you, and if you can love people, God will use you. It sure does change the dynamic when you walk in the doors. Now you are greeted by people you've done life with, prayed for and laughed with.

We live in a consumer obsessed society. So it makes sense that we would have a consumer mentality when it comes to church. We often expect everyone else, those who are "called" to be on staff or volunteer, to do the work of church. The rest of us enter, receive and leave. What we need to understand is, He calls all of us to give to others in some way. He gave us gifts and talents for a reason. May I be blunt? Church is not a gym or country club you belong to. Whether or not your church has "membership" is not the point. You will be blessed when you step out and give of yourself and others definitely will be blessed too.

I recently heard a message by T.D. Jakes where he was teaching on the story of the fig tree found in Mark 11:12. He talked about a God principle to "feed what feeds you." He explained that the tree was being fed by the ground around it and a healthy tree gives back fruit. It doesn't continue to take the water and nutrients from the earth without giving something in return. But isn't this the way many of us live our lives? We take, enjoy and move on.

This principle applies to personal and business relationships and to churches as well. Imagine being in a marriage and being the only person to give, to serve and to love. I hope this idea is unimaginable for you to comprehend, but for many of us, it feels like our experience. If you're living in a one-sided marriage, I'm so sorry. A healthy, blessed marriage, and any relationship for that matter, is one where both parties give to one another regularly. Where dreams, thoughts and ideas are received and discussed. A healthy church is one where the regular attenders give of their talents, time and financial resources. According to this principle, you should feed the church that feeds you. So, may I challenge you if you are not currently involved, take a step of faith and pray about what the Lord is leading you to do. Maybe even take a few minutes right now.

> *"Now (remember) this: He who sows sparingly and grudgingly will also reap sparingly and grudgingly, and he who sows generously (that blessings may come to someone) will also reap generously and with blessings."*
> 2 Corinthians 9:6 [AMP]

EQUILIBRIUM

Having said all of that, I have the feeling, if you've chosen to read this book, you're already involved with a local church. So, let's take a minute to address the other end of the spectrum. To all of my fellow church ladies: how many ministries are you serving in right now? How many nights a week are you at church? Ouch! Did that one hurt? I'm not sure why,

"Balance is tough to achieve and even harder to keep."

but it seems like much of the time people fall into one category or the other. Balance is tough to achieve and even harder to keep. People are either not involved at all or are over-committed. There usually isn't much middle ground. Personally, I have been on the terribly over-committed side of the scale, and let me tell you, the end result was a gradual decline to exhaustion.

Here's how it started. After high school, I attended Oral Roberts University. While at ORU, I met my husband, Michael, and after graduation, we moved back to Michigan, my home state. The Lord made sure we found our way to a small country church not far from where we lived. I had a professor that had a friend starting a church in my home town, who recommended we give it a try. My husband was a graduate assistant at ORU, and he had a student in one of his labs that coincidentally went to the same church. Her family helped us move our belongings back to Michigan, so we visited the church based on those recommendations and decided it was where the Lord wanted us. We made it our home and planted some roots—really deep roots.

I've always been a singer and love to worship, so the music ministry was the first ministry I joined (#1). Then, after a little while, we became Sunday school teachers (#2). The church started to grow and it was good. More years went by and we started a family. The church was still pretty small, so the unspoken rule was if you had kids in the nursery, you worked in the nursery, which made sense to me, so I worked in the nursery for years (#3). And the church continued to grow, and it was good. As the congregation grew, I no longer had to work in the nursery/kids area. Phew! However, occasionally new and necessary ministries were added to meet the needs of the people, and so did my level of involvement. Ministries like Partners-in-Prayer (#4), hospital visitation (#5), meals for those in need (#6), Life Groups (#7). You get the point. Crazy right? This is all while I had three young children at home and my husband often traveled for work. It was a gradual progression. I was like the frog in the pot that was starting to boil. Every time a new ministry was described to the congregation, I knew it was meeting a need, and I knew it was the will of the Father to meet all of these needs, so I joined. I don't remember praying much about it. I'm sure I must have to some degree, but the prayer, "Jesus, is this what you want me to be doing right now?" wasn't on my radar. At least, not that I remember.

Now, let me say this, God is merciful and gracious and really good. I did most of those things for many years with joy and was even energized by doing them. God is gracious, and the anointing of God brings supernatural provision, for sure. But now that I'm 25 years down the road, I can look at that and say to my younger self, "Girl, who are you trying to please?" At the time I would have said, "The Lord." (This answer will become one of the primary reasons for writing this book, but hold on, I will get to that later.) I would have admitted that, but I wouldn't have admitted that

I was trying to please my pastor, the leadership and many of those around me. I couldn't see it.

It has been my experience that most church leadership probably will never tell you that you're too involved and ask you to take a break from a ministry. I've personally never seen it happen. And actually, it's not their responsibility to keep track of everything you are involved in. That's on you, girlfriend, and me.

A few years ago, I heard Robert Morris, Pastor of Gateway Church in Texas, talk to a group of leaders at a conference I attended about the serving policy at his church. He talked about the problem of the same 20 percent of the congregation doing most, if not all, of the work. Pastor Robert understands and teaches the value of living a generous life. The idea that those who give and serve are as blessed as those who receive, actually more, is a concept that is littered throughout all of his messages and books. We are blessed when we give.

"Give, and it will be given to you. A good measure, pressed down shaken together and running over, will be poured into your lap." Luke 6:38

He told us that several years ago they implemented a policy that no one could serve in their church two weeks in a row. He mentioned his apprehension with this new policy because Gateway is huge, and it takes a lot of people to make it work. He told the group that much to his surprise, after the new policy, the number of volunteers increased. So they took it a step further and said there needed to be two weeks in-between each time you serve. Well, this must have resonated with the congregation because they practically had to turn people away. I'm not sure what their specific policy is currently, but I know if I went there, I could trust them with my gifts and talents. What an example this is. Pastor Robert, I applaud you, and if I'm ever in a position of leadership at this level, I will take my cue from you and be intentional about helping people maintain balance in their lives.

I used to think that every decision I made had to be forever. I guess that was because when I was younger, I was making those big life decisions: who to marry, what to study in college to prepare me for the career that God had called me to, where to settle down to start a family, etc. Those decisions are big, but other than who I am married to, they are all up for discussion these days. I am very deliberate with my children, who are all young adults, to make sure they do not put too much pressure on themselves to have everything figured out. Planning is good. (In fact, one of my favorite books is The Principle of the Path by Andy Stanley. Fantastic book. I think it should be mandatory reading for all middle school and high school students.) Yes, planning is good and seeking God first is even more necessary, but not every commitment needs to last 10 years to know you've heard from God. Some places are for a short season, while others are much longer. One is not more spiritually correct than the other. And that point takes me to my most recent church transition.

My husband and I worshiped at the little country church that eventually became a church of over a 1,000 until several years ago. We raised our children there, loved the people and the pastors there, and heard a deeper call from God for our lives there.

"But you, O Lord, are a shield for me, my glory and the lifter of my head." Psalm 3:3

LOOK UP

As a result of our involvement there, we rarely ever visited other churches. For years, maybe twenty, we only went to our church every Sunday and Wednesday night with the exception of a few church visits while on vacation and a few leadership conferences. Then circumstances with our children began to take us out. Looking back at the other church visits and messages from other pastors, it was like the Lord lifted my chin and said, "Look up, I'm doing something great in the world, and I want you to experience it too." Our first venture was to Hillsong Church in Sydney, Australia. Wow! What an experience! We took our oldest daughter there to attend their International Leadership College, and while we were there, we attended the Hillsong Conference. At this point, our lives and our church's perspective were very inward focused. It was all about what we were doing for God or at least what He was doing at our church. Brian Houston, the pastor of Hillsong, is very focused on the global "Church." His ministry is intentional about reaching the world with the gospel. You may be familiar with their worship music going back to Darlene Zschech's song, "Shout to the Lord" up to today's Hillsong United "Oceans". They have influenced worship all over the world and continue to do so today. Let's just say that global perspective was way out of my comfort zone, well at least with regards to how I saw myself. I was delighted they were making such an impact, but if you had asked me if I wanted to make a greater impact, I would have shied away, feeling like other people could do that, but not me. I'm just a housewife from Michigan. What could I do that would change the world? Can you relate?

The next year, we visited a church in Kalamazoo Michigan where our daughter was hired as a graphic designer and served as a worship leader. I remember while visiting one Sunday, during service, the pastors recognized a woman's birthday. She was a volunteer who had given much time and energy to the work of the Lord there. She stood and sheepishly waved to the very large congregation. They acknowledged and blessed her and she sat down. This may be no big deal to you, but I was crying. I looked at my friend who was with me and she was crying. Crazy right? It was the simplicity of the gospel in action. I just loved how these people honored one another and how they weren't afraid to acknowledge each other. The pastors understood that you don't have to recognize everyone, they couldn't possibly with so many people, but when you see people and honor them, everyone is honored.

One last example of the Lord lifting my chin to "look up" was at a leadership conference. Rick Bezet from New Life Church in Conway, Arkansas was one of the speakers. I don't remember the jokes he told, the topic of his message, or the scriptures he referenced, but I do remember the amazing anointing of love that flowed from this man. My husband and I waited after the service to thank him and shake his hand, and so did a lot of other people. Not wanting to be in the way, we stood off to the side and waited. He greeted people for so long that the church liaisons were ready to whisk him off to lunch.

"I'm just a house-wife from Michigan. What can I do to change the world?"

He had to be very tired and hungry, but he saw us, and he told them lunch could wait just a minute longer. Through tears we thanked him for his heart. This man was so full of the love of Christ, we were overwhelmed. It was embarrassing. Geesh! We couldn't even talk. I'm crying again now, writing this, remembering how this man knows the Lord. I want to know Him like that too. What a glimpse we got that day of the Father's love and compassion for us. I want to know the love of God in a deeper way. That is the cry of my heart. In Ephesians 3:17-19 Paul writes, *"And I pray that you, being rooted and established in love, may have power, together with all the saints, to grasp how wide and*

20

long and high and deep is the love of Christ, and to know this love that surpasses knowledge - that you may be filled to the measure of all the fullness of God." That is my prayer for you today as well. That you would grasp ahold of this amazing love that is being poured on you and that you would be filled to overflowing, just like Rick was, to spill on those around you today.

DON'T DIE IN THE NEST

As time went on, and through a series of circumstances that I won't bore you with, God began to reveal himself to my husband and me in a much greater way. He began calling and stretching us, and we began entertaining the idea that maybe it was time for us to move on. After being at our church for approximately 24 years, you can imagine what an excruciating process that was. We were devoted not only to the Lord but to the people and the ministry there. Looking back, I can see how our level of devotion was unhealthy. We really weren't open to what God wanted us to do because it was the culture of our church that if you're committed to the Lord and the church, you didn't leave. My heart began to break, but the drawing of the Lord was greater than my motives for staying.

We had been praying about the decision to seek another church for about two years when I finally asked the Lord to "knock me over the head with a 2x4 if He had something else for us." That 2x4 came within the week by one of the many spiritual voices I had placed myself under. While watching one of the recorded services from the Potter's House, Bishop T.D. Jakes preached a message called "Don't Die in the Nest." I knew the moment I heard it that his message was the answer to my prayer. I think I even had a bump on my head to prove it.

I love how personal God is. He blows me away with His ability to speak a specific word to many different people using one message. In the message, Bishop Jakes talked about the habits of the eagle and described in very compelling detail how the mother eagle builds her nest for her young. She makes it sturdy and lines it with feathers to make it a warm, safe environment for her babies. He talked about how good it was for the eaglets while they grew and thrived there. Then he began to tell of how the mother begins to stir the nest to make the babies progressively more and more uncomfortable. Well, if that was not my experience, I don't know what was. It was time to leave this place where I had matured and grown into an eagle that was now ready to fly.

I've heard people describe that sometimes there is grace for something, and then without warning, God removes the grace to be there and you know it's time to make a change. This can apply to a job, a relationship or even a church. The process of leaving ours should have been easier than it was, but God used that painful experience to reveal His amazing, great love to me. He had something better for me, and in my desire to remain faithful, I would have missed it if

He had not allowed hurt and pain to come my way. Desperation is useful in the kingdom of God. It lifts our head quicker than any other thing, and boy was I desperate.

What's The Point?

📖 Read Acts 2

* What is your main takeaway from this chapter?

* As believers we make up the capital "C" Church. This body of believers is global and includes everyone who calls Jesus Christ Lord all around the world. It doesn't have walls or a building. We are the building. When we get together, love and serve each other, we are a light that shines in the darkness of this world. If we are already the body of Christ, why is it necessary to gather together locally?

* The body is made up of individual parts (1 Corinthians 12). Thinking about your talents, desires and even the things that you are passionate about, what part(s) of the body would you consider yourself?

* Are you contributing to the body as much as you could?

* Is the Lord dealing with you about stepping out into a new area of service or ministry?

* Acts 2 gives us a picture of what the first church looked like. What would you say was their "secret weapon"? (Hint: Acts 2:38 and Romans 8:9-11)

"Every day they continued to meet together in the temple courts. They broke bread in their homes and ate together with glad and sincere hearts, praising God and enjoying the favor of all the people. And the Lord added to their number daily those who were being saved."
Acts 2:46-47

SUGGESTED READING
_____

The Best Yes by Lisa Terkeurst

2

Confession:
I've Been Hurt by the Church

"A new command I give you: Love one another. As I have loved you so you must love one another. By this all men will know that you are my disciples, if you love one another."
John 13:34-35

I thought I was crazy. I thought I had a bad heart. I thought I was the only one. I wasn't and I didn't, but that is often the mentality of people who have been in an unhealthy environment for any length of time.

We had been at our church for over 24 years, and the Lord was stirring us and drawing us to something new. He was exposing us to new ideas and ways of thinking and expanding our knowledge of His great love for us. It was time for us to move on, but we weren't sure how to do it. Others that had left our church were labeled offended, misguided or even disobedient, so we knew it was going to be a challenge to leave well. Naively, we hoped that after serving alongside them for 24 years, our pastors and the leadership would know our hearts and treat our leaving differently. They didn't.

But before I continue, let me say that this is a very difficult chapter for me to write. It was the darkest, most difficult season of my life, and I know that sharing this part of my story will be the most challenging because it must be done with grace and discretion. I know that God takes seriously what we say about His own and I'm glad because that means He's concerned with what people say about me too. James 3:17 says, *"But the wisdom that comes from heaven is first of all pure; then peace-loving, considerate, submissive, full of mercy and good fruit, impartial and sincere. Peacemakers who sow in peace raise a harvest of righteousness."* I love that. That's good advice right there. Advice I try to live my life by and definitely advice that is guiding the writing of this book. It is only by the grace of God that I can look at this very painful experience with peace and forgiveness in my heart. He has brought healing to my soul. He has spoken to me through His Word time and time again, bringing instruction, confirmation, correction, guidance, and a Kingdom perspective to my situation and my life. I

"I discovered that because my heart was hurt, it didn't mean I was offended or overly sensitive. Just human."

know that the Bible says if we seek Him we will find Him. I now have a greater revelation of that truth. And if He will do it for me, I know He will do it for you.

So it is with humility and trepidation that I recall the events of the past couple of years. It is my objective to *"speak the truth in love"* as found in Ephesians 4:15. Having said all of that, you may be asking yourself: *Why write about your hurt if you have to go to all of the trouble to preface it? Wouldn't it honor God more not to talk about it?* Isn't it like when you hear someone say, "I really shouldn't tell you this but..."? I always try to stop people when they say that to me because I don't want to hear it if I don't need to hear it. So, for me, not talking about something difficult used to always be the best option. James 1:19 says, *"Be quick to listen, slow to speak and slow to become angry."* Words to live by; however, never questioning, never speaking about anything negative or difficult, never addressing any unhealthy issue was the culture that contributed to the dysfunction in our church and in my life. For me, the answer was clear as to why I needed to write this because for years I felt like I was crazy. I felt bad about feeling bad, if that makes any sense. And it wasn't until I read about other people's journeys and what other people had experienced that I began to find healing. Discovering that I was not alone helped me. Discovering that because my heart was hurt didn't mean I was offended or overly sensitive, just human. And hearing someone say, "It's not ok," gave me permission to ask

God what I should do. Should I stay and continue to cover the dysfunction and love people, or was it ok to ask the Lord if He wanted to take us somewhere else? If you've never been in a high control atmosphere, you may not have any idea what I'm talking about, and I hope that is your experience, but if you have been or continue to be, perhaps you might be prompted to pray and ask God for guidance for your own situation. Either way, in an effort to bring healing to others, I will continue.

LEAVE WELL

When we went to our pastor and his wife and discussed our desire to leave and to leave well, we asked them how to do it. We wanted to know what that looked like to them. They could not give us an answer. We offered to step down from ministries slowly or quickly. We were open to their suggestions as to how to articulate our leaving and placed ourselves in their hands one last time, but they could not offer us any advice. They had made it pretty clear throughout the years and at our meeting that leaving to go somewhere else, especially in the area, was wrong. I guess they didn't feel the Lord would call you to another fellowship. I guess that's where I got that mentality from. For years, I felt bad for even contemplating that the Lord might be calling us to another place. Now I realize that what we learned from our pastors and leaders, and what we gave that fellowship was great, but incomplete to what the Lord had for us. Simply put, it was time to move on. In an effort to avoid potential wrath, we had contemplated moving out-of-state the year before we actually left our church because we wanted to maintain relationship with the congregation. But we did not have peace about it, so we attempted to do it the "normal" way, which in our situation was the *hard* way. Still, in need of godly direction, my husband researched the topic. We thought about going to another respected leader in our area for advice, but we knew in order to get council we would have to give them details about our situation, and we didn't want to talk to others about what we felt was unhealthy in our leaders and environment. Looking back, I think it would have been a wise choice. We were not only in need of council but unbeknownst to us at the time, ministry as well. I know that God honors us when we honor Him and each other, so we took the advice we read in articles written by respected pastors and church leaders online. The advice we took was to be 'all in and then leave quickly.' That's what we did.

Obviously, we are not "church hoppers." That was one of the labels placed on people who left, but I think 24 years at the same church takes care of that label. We were not offended—another label given—because from my experience, people who leave because they are offended typically do it within the first 2-3 times they are offended. I remember a conversation I had with a woman many years ago. She had just joined our choir and I was asking her about her life. She started to tell me right away why she had left her previous church. She told me about what someone had said or done (I can't remember the details), but long story short, she let me know that they offended her and she left. I told her if she were looking for a church where she wouldn't get offended she'd better leave this one. She looked at me with shock. I then went on to tell her how every church is full of people, and people will hurt your feelings and say stupid things. I expressed that relationships are messy, but if she were willing to love people and work through difficult situations with people, she would love it here. I can't remember if she stayed or not, but my intention was to speak the truth in love to her. The truth is, she probably left because I offended her. I understand that no church is perfect and there are no perfect people. If we had left because we were looking for the perfect place or because someone offended one of us, we would have never stayed for 24 years. People offend us and we offend people. It happens. My philosophy on the whole thing, and I believe God's Word supports this, is to give people the benefit of the doubt and chose to not be offended—to quickly forgive and to quickly ask for forgiveness. That has worked well for me in my marriage, with my kids and friends, with everyone I have relationship with.

> *"I've heard it said that the harder it is to leave a church, the more unhealthy it is."*

I've heard it said that the harder it is to leave a church, the more unhealthy it is. Well, it was next to impossible to leave mine, so I'll let you draw your own conclusion.

This, however, does not undo all of the wonderful things that happened while we were there. For most of the years, the good far outweighed the bad. It had to; otherwise, we wouldn't have stayed as long as we did. Our children had ownership of their own church experience from a very young age, meaning they did not go to church because we made them. They were involved in serving at church very early on, so if we had to miss, they were upset because they had people they wanted to see and people who were counting on them. I'm convinced that if you love to serve at church as an extension of your love for the Lord, your children will catch that. Ours did. I had the privilege of being one of the worship leaders for many years, and we had amazing times of rejoicing, worshiping and basking in the Lord's presence corporately. The Word was preached and prayer was a priority. I learned a lot. My husband and I were involved in several small groups that brought much joy and fulfillment to our lives. Having the opportunity to get to do life with people is the greatest gift we are given. We celebrated marriages, new babies, graduations, and we ministered faith and love to each other in times of sickness. Sadly, we also mourned several deaths together. The friendships we made during our time there are precious, and as far as we are concerned are for life.

That's why leaving these dear people and the church we helped to grow was so bittersweet. I wish so badly that we could have been "blessed out" so to speak, so we didn't have to totally sever relationship. I had hoped to be the exception and to be able to visit and continue to have relationship. In our eyes we continued to be family, still part of the body, the C Church. However, that was not possible even though I tried. It is why being shunned by the leadership, staff and many in the congregation was so painful. It was by far the most painful time in my life. Sorry, I already said that.

You may be asking yourself, *Were you Amish?* No. *Are you a Scientologist?* No. *Do people still shun people?* Yep, they do. They don't call it that. They tell people to 'separate themselves from toxic people or attitudes.' They tell people 'if you continue in relationship with them, you are not loyal to us.' For years I believed this message and even participated in what I would call shunning by non-pursuit. If and when people would leave, I didn't ask why. I didn't reach out. People I loved and respected left and I just let them go counting on the message given by leadership as truth. The messages were almost always negative on the part of those leaving. They wanted more influence. They were offended. They were presumptuous. They had a bad attitude. Whatever. There was not usually an effort (that I could see) to help people grow past an offense, for leadership to take any responsibility for handling disagreements badly, or an effort made to help people find a place where they could utilize their gifts and talents when it wasn't a natural, easy fit. I can see now how my inactivity hurt people. Now, I wish I would have reached out to them if only to say, "Lord bless you. You will be missed." I felt like I wasn't supposed to know their reasoning because being sympathetic or even just talking about anything negative would be misunderstood as being in agreement. I'm sure some of the people who left simply felt called to another place. But as I've stated, I wouldn't really know if that was their reasoning because I never asked, and in our culture, God calling you to another fellowship was not something God would do. Looking back, and talking with others currently, I'm amazed that was my mentality.

I recall a time when I said to a friend at church, "I will never leave… (my former church). I wasn't even open to God's voice in this regard. I believe now that is why He allowed some really painful things to happen to us. It had to get *ugly* before we could/would hear His voice in this regard. It was to our benefit it got difficult. The phrase "pain brings change" comes to mind. I no longer hold this "lifer" perspective about church. I am led by the Holy Spirit. Where He leads me, I will go. I hold on to people and places loosely, and I am open to whatever the Lord wants me to do.

Many of our close friends were made to choose, which was excruciating for them and painful for us. I can say now, after many years, the shunning, or ghosting as some call it, is not as bad as it was. Most people talk to me if they run into me and many even go out of their way to let me know that they love and miss us. I always really appreciate that. Unfortunately, some members and my former pastors *still* go out of their way to avoid us and others who have left, on purpose. I don't get it. We don't have to be fake and act like nothing ever happened, but wouldn't it be nice to say "hello" and shake a hand or give a hug? It would have been so much better if we could have left with our pastors' blessing. It would have been so much better for us … and for them.

I must confess, I understand some people are difficult to please. People want what they want or feel they deserve, and they don't take the vision of the church or the responsibility to the many vs. the needs of the one into account. I get that. Pastors have it tough trying to please everyone. However, just because this is true about people, it doesn't excuse the abusive behavior described in this chapter in any way.

Recently, my mom was talking to me about marriage and told me about her 85/15 rule. She said if your marriage is 85% positive and 15% dealing with difficult issues, you're doing well. No one has a 100% trouble free, enjoyable marriage. That sounds reasonable to me. It also makes me think about the process of leaving our church. No place is perfect; no people are perfect. The unhealthy portion seemed to be only the 15% in the early years, but as time went by, the dysfunction (in my experience), appeared to increase until the numbers were reversed by the time we left.

I hate the pain our leaving has caused my former pastor and his wife. I know it was painful for them because of the aching and anger they expressed when other people left. They even struggled to let a team go plant a church out-of-state, an endeavor that included their children and was supported and partially funded by the church. From my perspective, this should have been a joyous occasion. Isn't that the goal? To raise people up to continue the ministry of the gospel? I get the difficult emotions that come when your grown children leave to live their own lives, but the grief expressed seemed excessive and unhealthy. My desire to avoid the obvious pain this team's departure brought caused us to stay longer than we should have. My heart still hurts when I consider that when my former pastors think of us, they might feel betrayal, pain or anger. They are great people, and I learned a lot from them. Hurting them personally and damaging the church in any way was the absolute last thing we wanted to do.

I say 'damaged' because based on what I've heard from those who remain, that is the message that was communicated. We didn't encourage anyone to leave, ever. As a matter of fact, there were a few people that asked us if they should leave because they too saw the unhealthiness, but we encouraged them to stay. We emphasized that they needed to hear from God regarding their specific situation. However, considering the culture, our leaving may have opened the door so to speak. Personally, I don't think we damaged the church by leaving. I think if it gave people permission to seek God about His will for their life or made it acceptable to evaluate how leadership was behaving, then that was a good thing.

SPIRITUAL ABUSE IS DEVASTATING

I've used the term spiritual abuse. You may be asking yourself, "What does that really look like? What do you mean by spiritual abuse? Can I say first, that I am personally uncomfortable with the term 'spiritual abuse'? Not because I doubt it's real, but because it is not at all something I want to be associated with and never thought would happen to me. As I write this, I'm asking myself why talking about abuse makes me so uncomfortable? I guess it's for three reasons: One, I was trained for 25 years not to question authority or talk about negative feelings/behavior. Two, I've heard people throw the term around about their pastors because they don't like their leadership or communication style (poor leadership and/or personal preference is not spiritual abuse). And three, most pastors and leaders are not abusive! They love deeply, they sacrifice daily and they bring healing and encouragement to the people around them. I absolutely respect anyone who says "yes" to the call. I understand the pressures that push from all sides on a pastor's wife. I speak to this issue with trepidation because of all of the selfless, sacrificing, God honoring saints that serve the local church worldwide. But for the sake of the wounded I will detail some of the factors that can make up a spiritually abusive culture. To bring understanding and healing to the outcast or separated one, I will continue on this very uncomfortable journey and write.

I know it's cliché, but it's true. Hurting people hurt people, and many people have been hurt by the church, and have not allowed the Lord to bring restoration and healing to their lives, and this includes pastors. Many leaders have been mentored and raised up in controlling, abusive atmospheres, so they learn to lead from a place of control and insecurity. This type of leadership is damaging in so many ways. It fosters a culture of fear and judgment. It allows for angry and unkind top-down communication to be acceptable. I recall messages that were given passively from the pulpit or in small group settings that continually addressed that leadership, "anointed authority" is not to be questioned. That fathers correct sons, but sons never correct fathers, and those with callings or dreams that are not sanctioned by authority are in some way unfaithful or not submitted to leadership, and indirectly to the Lord. I learned early on to not be too assertive with my thoughts and ideas. I learned to keep my head down, do what others told me to do without questioning and serve no matter

> *"Spiritual abuse is real, and it hurts you at the deepest core of who you are."*

the impact on my family or peace of mind. This type of culture is abusive and is confusing and heartbreaking when you experience it. So, for the sake of discussion and possible healing, I will push past my discomfort and speak the truth in love as I know it.

Spiritual abuse is real, and it hurts you to the deepest core of who you are. We are spirits housed in a body, and a wound to our spirit can be even more devastating than a physical one. My good friend endured physical abuse at the hand of a family member as a child for years, and she shared with me that the pain of the spiritual abuse she experienced at the hands of church leadership was greater than what she endured as a child. When you are abused physically, it's easy to define as wrong. No one is going to argue with you about how it damages or affects you, but spiritual abuse is so much more nebulous. The devil likes to use our strengths against us. Our commitment, loyalty and desire to "do" something for the Lord are positive qualities that can be used against us when we are in an abusive environment. Abusive leaders will take advantage of extremely loyal or faithful people, serving their own needs or the needs of their ministry above the needs and health of the individual. I would like to remind us, the devil is sneaky and he is the real enemy. Chapter eight discusses this in greater detail, but it's important that we recognize that people, even those who wound and abuse are not the enemy, the devil is.

This is what I know to be true regarding abuse, both spiritual and physical: secrets make you sick. When people tell a trusted friend about abusive circumstances, it can set them free. The shame of that offense begins to lose its grip the moment you share it, bringing it into the light. It also can bring healing, because when you tell your story, others who suffer from a similar shame begin to realize that they are not alone. Your testimony can bring healing, hope and restoration to others.

I am by no means an expert on the topic of physical or spiritual abuse, but I have learned some things along the way. In an article by Dayna Drum in *Relevant Magazine* she says, "It [abuse] can be subtle or painfully loud - anything from unquestioned pastoral authority, to practices of shaming members if they don't fulfill religious expectations, to badmouthing members who have left."[1]

All of these were evident in my situation. This is not ok. If you are attending a church that has an oppressive atmosphere where authority has no checks and balances, you don't have to stay if it leads to unchecked hurtful behavior. If the leader of your ministry makes you feel bad or "punishes" you socially or emotionally when you need to step down for a season, or even for good, that's not ok. If your pastor knows about it and allows it to continue, that's not ok either. If people are not free to leave without being labeled, it's not ok. Sometimes the Lord is moving us from one place to another, one ministry to another.

If we are not free to obey His voice without guilt and shame, it's just not ok.

Having said that, it is also not right to leave a church badly. Talking about everything that needs improvement to others or expressing your dissatisfaction regarding the policies or personalities does not honor God—and using Facebook to air dirty laundry or debate theology is never productive. We didn't do everything right, I'm sure not even close, but I can honestly tell you that no one at church, including our children, knew we were contemplating leaving. We did not talk bad about people, we really tried to keep a good attitude, and no one knew that the Lord was dealing with us about going somewhere else. However, because we were in positions of influence, our leaving was a shock to people, so we did end up having to give some details to close friends when they asked us why we left. There were others that were experiencing a stirring to leave, and when we "opened the door" by leaving, so to speak, they left too. We tried to focus on the positive aspects of our departure—simply, that God had something else for us, and He did. He wanted to do a new thing in us and He was taking us to a new place to do it.

Let me be very clear. Please do not miss this. I am not saying that every time we experience conflict or disagreements at church we *should* leave. It's healthier to stay and address a difficult situation as we are called to prayerfully and humbly speak the truth in love. If you are able to address a situation and resolve it peacefully and there is not a pattern of leadership hurting or abusing people, staying is always a good choice! Matthew 18:15 communicates this. *"If your brother sins against you, go and show him his fault, just between the two of you. If he listens to you, you have won your brother over."* I will confess, however, I did stay hoping to affect change. I have recently learned that trying to change someone else, even if I think it will help people, is manipulation. I will own that. I'm not doing that any more.

In an effort to help us understand spiritual abuse better, here are a few signs of spiritual abuse I found in an article on Facebook written by Alan Smith, Senior Pastor of Catch The Fire Church in Dallas/Fort Worth, Texas. They will help you determine whether or not you are in a healthy environment. Prayerfully consider this information. If you are a pastor reading this or are in church leadership, may I respectfully ask you to let the Lord search your heart to see if there is anything He would like to address in your ministry?

"Search me, O God, and know my heart; test me and know my anxious thoughts. See if there is any offensive way in me, and lead me in the way everlasting."
Psalm 139:23-24

(I have added my thoughts inside Pastor Alan's quote in italics to illustrate these ideas.)

In his post about spiritual abuse on
October 13, 2014 Pastor Alan said:

It is not safe to question authority.
*If you disagree or question authority, you may "pay the price."
You may get a cold shoulder, an angry response, or leader-
ship may threaten to take ministry opportunities from you.*

**Authority plays the God card to manipulate
and control.**
*Church structure/spiritual authority is addressed often. "Don't
touch the Lord's anointed" and other similar phrases are used to
separate and elevate leadership from the rest of the church body.*

**Authority enforces rules they are themselves
exempt from.**
*The congregation is expected to give grace and cover for shortcomings
and/or failures of leaders, but it is not reciprocated. Those under
authority will most likely "pay the price" for their bad choices.*

**Authority controls the story narrative by
making sure you have limited contact or influence from those who would tell a different
story.**
*When we left, we wrote a letter to our pastors sharing with
them how God was calling us elsewhere. They had a meeting
with the congregation and told them what we said (with
editing) in place of reading the letter, which didn't allow
for others to hear our hearts. They controlled the message.*

Those who leave are labeled in some way and then shunned relationally.

Sometimes it is communicated directly and other times passively to avoid and not speak with people who have left. It is also considered disloyal to ask why someone has left. People who leave are labeled as "toxic."

If I may, let me break one of these down for you to explain the subtle way it affects you. "It is not safe to question authority." I like that Pastor Alan uses the word "safe." I remember a meeting that happened approximately 20 years ago. I was with a group of my peers, and we were all instructed to come up with a Bible study for our small group using our pastor's wife's Bible study as our guide. Evidently, I strayed too far from her message, and this made her angry. I was used in a meeting as an example of what not to do. My study was tossed across the table to me, and I was asked on the spot to defend my reasons for including the material I put in my study. The room was quiet, and I'm not sure we all knew where her frustration was coming from. I know I didn't. Her anger seemed disproportionate to my "offense." (I can take correction. It was not my heart to be out of line or rebellious. I do, however, remember trying to be creative with my study as the study guide provided had already been taught once. She had every opportunity to mention her dissatisfaction to me privately about what I needed to change, but she didn't.) She waited until we were all together, so this wasn't correction; this was shaming and was used to warn me and others what not to do. The women and I sat there stunned. As I attempted to recall my reasoning for the content I included months earlier, it was apparent that no explanation was going to appease her. The room was silent. So quiet I was sure those sitting next to me could hear my heart beating, as I felt like it would explode at any moment. No one dared speak up in my defense, as they knew they would be next. A few apologized to me later for not *helping* me, but I understood why they didn't. I explained my decisions the best I could under the circumstances, as I sat in shock and shame. It was not at all in my heart to be uncooperative or "stiff-necked."

After the meeting, I sat alone, stunned at what just happened. I spoke to my leader privately and told her how embarrassed I was. I told her unapologetically that I was shocked that she handled the situation so publicly. The following week I was called to a meeting with her, and she spoke firmly to me that if I ever "pushed back" like that again when confronted with correction I would no longer be allowed to lead my small group. I loved leading my small group, but I got the message loud and clear. It was not safe to question authority or to defend myself no matter the reason. I learned that if I challenged or questioned authority, the ministry/ministries I am called to and love would be taken from me, and I would be shamed in front of my peers. It's interesting; I'm really not very good at remembering conversations and situations, but boy, I remember very well the pain, embarrassment, and shame that came to my heart that day. I did everything I could to avoid those emotions from then on. I kept my head down, stayed within the lines, and learned that it was not safe to speak up, take initiative or defend myself.

I recently listened to a great podcast on *Healing from Spiritual Abuse* by Mark and Melissa DeJesus on YouTube. In their discussion they mention that the first step to receiving healing from abuse is the ability to recognize it. I would agree with that. It wasn't until I read about what others had to say about the topic that I found the courage to describe my experience as abusive. Mark and Melissa give 14 signs of Spiritual Abuse. (As I conclude this chapter, take this information and add it to what's already been given, and ask the Holy Spirit to reveal truth to your heart and mind.) Mark begins by stating, "The goal for the enemy is to use spiritual abuse to divide the unified body of Christ, and to keep it from being the family is was meant to be, and leave people so wounded that they are rendered ineffective because they have been 'taken out' so badly."[2]

The following are my notes from their discussion on the signs of Spiritual Abuse. (YouTube: #158: Healing from Spiritual Abuse: Part 2)

- **Honor, respect and authority are distorted:** People cannot talk about issues because you can't touch the Lord's anointed. The culture does not allow for those under authority to "speak up" regarding difficult issues or anything negative.

- **It is an unsafe environment:** People are labeled, embarrassed and/or ridiculed by leadership. Not allowed to agree to disagree.

- **Performance driven culture:** Big focus on image. People are viewed as commodities to further the church's cause. Behavior and service are valued over heart, which requires endless and exhausting involvement for the people.

- **Fear and shame drive people into submission:** Punish by shame. Public confrontations and discipline when it's not necessary to do so.

- **Major emphasis is placed on a charismatic leader:** The Pastor(s) are the supreme authority, not allowing for individual thoughts from staff, leaders or members.

- **Leader's sin issues or weaknesses are minimized while others are maximized:** Messages are designed to manipulate, passively addressing issues. There is very little vulnerability and humility from those in authority. Leaders are not trained on repenting or apologizing.

- **Leaders over-spiritualize:** What is said is directly from God all of the time so no one can object or question it. This makes it difficult if things don't work out, to make changes or just be honest about it. Pride is usually the root behind this.

- **Over-involvement in congregation's personal decisions:** People feel obliged to ask the pastor for his/her permission or blessing when making personal decisions about a major decision like a job change or move.

- **Exclusive spirituality:** God is only showing us or speaking to our church. Not willing to collaborate or reach out to other churches.

- **Financial manipulation:** People receive based on what they give. Mis-use of funds.

- **Internal bubble:** Members are discouraged from interacting with family members who do not attend.

- **Unwillingness to act with compassion for those who leave:** Shunning, ghosting is evident. People have a fear of leaving. They don't want what happened to "them" to happen to me.

- **Isolated accountability to leaders:** No healthy debate. No challenging discussions or healthy dialogue-leading to a "clone" environment.

- **Strong legalism, religious pressure:** Outward appearance is more important than what's going on inside. Subliminal message-do better, do more.

So yes, I have experienced many of the signs of spiritual abuse that Pastor Alan and the DeJesus' describe. The great news is, God has brought great healing to those wounded places in my soul and spirit. He continues to love me, forgive me, reveal truth to me and heal the tender wounds of my past. I am required to forgive and repent for the things that I have done to hurt others. I am required to walk in humility and to check my motives and my heart's attitude, and just when I think I am healed, He continues to reveal a hurt or wrong mindset and brings greater healing and restoration to my soul.

I've heard it said that personal growth is often preceded by hardship. I would absolutely agree. I am so grateful for what God has done in my thinking, my heart and my relationship with Him. I've heard people who have battled cancer or gone through a horrendous trial say that if they had it to do over, they wouldn't change a thing. When I heard this, I would say to myself, "Are you crazy? Why would you not want to get out of going through that if you could?" Well, now I understand. When I was empty, He filled me. When I was desperate, He met me. When I was lonely, He wrapped His arms around me. When I was down, He picked me up and set my feet on a rock. This "Death of a Church Lady" season in my life, when God was peeling everything back and allowing me to understand who I am in Him, was *hard but good*. It continues to be hard but good. Learning to live from grace, not for grace, was just the beginning for me. Looking back, I see His grace and mercy covering me like a shield, and I can honestly say "I know Him more" as a result of the events of the past several years, and that has always been the cry of my heart. The rest of this book is about the *how* He has healed my heart. I pray it will bring healing to you as well as you journey with me.

GOD IS SPEAKING. CAN YOU HEAR HIM?

Not long after I left my church, I attended a Freedom Ministry training. This week was devoted to learning how to hear the voice of God personally in a greater way, and it was a monumental time of healing. Something happened on the first day that articulates the hand of God in my life during that devastating time. We did an exercise where we had to find someone we did not know and pair up with them. Then we had to look into their eyes for two minutes. Two whole minutes! That's a long time to look into a stranger's eyes. That's a long time to look into anyone's eyes. I thought, *Have I ever gazed into my husband's eyes for that long?* Not without laughing, that's for sure. Anyway, after the awkward time was up, he had us do it again. Only this time we had an assignment. We were to ask the Lord what He would want to say to our partner if we were willing to be used as a vessel. This second time, with my new assignment, I was praying for her, waiting on God and hoping to have a word of encouragement or direction for her. As he was counting down … 10, 9, 8, 7 … I was saying to myself, *Wait, I need more time. Is this what you want to say to her Lord?* The time flew by. It really was remarkable. My word for her was simple, not super spiritual. I saw a Nike swoosh and told her to "Just do it!" She laughed a little and said she had an idea what it might be referring to and would pray about it. No big revelation there, but her word for me was amazing. I had never met this woman. In fact, we had only been at the seminar for a few hours, but God used her to tell me that I was not alone, that He had me in His hands. She began to speak and I began to cry. She said, "I see you, and the Lord is holding you with His arms outstretched, and you are dangling like a limp rag doll in His arms. He wants me to tell you that He picked you up over here and put you over there. He did this for you because you couldn't/wouldn't have been able to get there by yourself." Well, that was it. I knew that God saw me and was aware of my pain, but that picture was so spot on and articulated how I felt so well during that time that I often thank Him for that image and the confirmation that I am currently exactly where I am supposed to be. I had been asking God if I had done the right thing and had we settled at the right church. He is faithful to confirm when we ask, and I knew that He was in it all. I knew I was at the right place. My new pastor, Jim Weigand, says, "God never wastes." I love that. And I agree.

What's The Point?

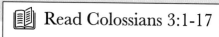

📖 Read Colossians 3:1-17

* What is your main takeaway from this chapter?

* Whether we like it or not, if we live in this world and we are in relationship with people, we are going to be hurt, and odds are, we will also hurt others. The question is, what are we going to do about it?

* How does this chapter speak to your experience with church?

* It's important to not rush past this chapter. Take some time to allow the Holy Spirit to speak to you. Perhaps He will point out an abusive behavior you have been unintentionally inflicting on others. Maybe He will highlight in your spirit the way(s) you have been abused. We can't change something we are not aware of. This could be the first step toward healing and forgiveness.

* What do you hear the Spirit saying to you regarding the issue of spiritual abuse?

* Is there someone you need to forgive? Remember, forgiveness doesn't mean it was ok. It means that you are willing to let God be the judge and you no longer hold on to the event(s) that hurt you or your loved ones.

* Do you need to apologize to someone? Are you willing to humble yourself and ask for forgiveness?

* What boundaries, if any, do you need to set in place in order to get healthy?

* I know several people who have given up on church. They are no longer willing to put themselves at risk. If that's you, keep reading, friend. The devil wants to isolate you. He wants to keep you where you're at. Please don't listen to him. God has so much more for you. The rest of this book is my journey to healing and freedom. It is my prayer, as you read about what God has done for me and in me, that you too will hear His voice and be different than you were when you started. Trust Him to bring healing and freedom to the broken places in your heart.

"Therefore, as God's chosen people, holy and dearly loved, clothe yourselves with compassion, kindness, humility, gentleness and patience. Bear with each other and forgive whatever grievances you may have against one another. Forgive as the Lord forgave you. And over all these virtues put on love, which binds them all together in perfect unity."
Colossians 3:12-13

SUGGESTED READING

Healing Your Church Hurt
by Stephen Mansfield

3

Confession:
I Love to Laugh

"A merry heart does good like a medicine,
but a crushed spirit dries up the bones."
Proverbs 17:22 (KJV)

My mother-in-law once called me the "laugh-ing-est woman she knows." I figure if you are going to be known for something, laughing isn't too bad—as long as you don't laugh like Janice on *Friends* or Steve Urkel on *Family Matters*. I do have a throw-your-head-back, hear-it-anywhere-in-the-room cackle. It runs in the family. But doesn't it feel good to laugh? To laugh until you cry or your side aches. I love to laugh!

Proverbs 17:22 is one of my favorite scriptures. Depending on what version of the Bible you are reading, several different words are used in place of merry—cheerful, joyful, rejoicing. A rejoicing heart. Doesn't that sound like something you want to have? I do. Some people are just naturally cheerful. I know this sweet young lady named Melody, and she is always cheerful. I'm sure she has her off days, but I imagine even then she is pleasant. I have never seen her in a bad mood or heard her say a negative thing. Then you have those people who just always seem sour. "Having a nice day, Mr. Jones?" "I would if it wasn't so windy. Blah, blah, blah…" But I think most of us fall somewhere in between. For the most part, we are pretty cheerful, but often we allow our moods and circumstances to dictate our heart's perspective, and as we know, that can be dangerous because we are warned to guard our heart. The scripture in Proverbs 17 goes on to say, *"a crushed spirit dries up the bones."* Wow! So, a cheerful heart is good like a medicine and a crushed or broken spirit dries up the bones. Dry bones are dead bones. We see this mentioned in Ezekiel 37:4, *"Prophecy to these bones and say to them, 'O dry bones, hear the word of the Lord'…"* Ezekiel was in a valley where an army had been defeated and died there. All that was left of the men were their dry, dead bones. Sometimes terrible things happen to us or are done to us, and our spirit gets crushed. Life happens. It's happened to me. The process of allowing God to touch those places and

"A good laugh can release endorphins, the body's feel-good chemicals."

bring comfort, healing and His great love helps to relieve the pain. If I allow Him and seek Him, the Lord can bring life to that crusty, dry place. If I keep my pain to myself and "lick the wound," so to speak, the dry edges can spread to the whole area and soon there is a hardening that occurs. It's interesting to me that these two thoughts are put together, but I think the concept of a merry/rejoicing heart is the antidote or remedy to a crushed spirit. So again, we are presented with a choice. Do we want medicine to keep our heart healthy, or do we want to dry up and get old before our time? What if we spoke to our soul like Ezekiel spoke life to those bones? "Rejoice, soul." "Look for the positive, mind." "Keep the faith, heart." There will be plenty of time in the following chapters to deal with difficult issues like spiritual warfare, fear and surrender. For now, let's rejoice and laugh a little. While we're at it, let's bring a little sunshine into the lives of the people we encounter today.

Laughter is good like a medicine. I always feel better after a good laugh. It's pretty well documented that laughter strengthens your immune system, helps to diminish pain and reduces stress. A good laugh can release endorphins, the body's feel-good chemicals. Laughter relaxes us and helps us put things into the right perspective. The emotions we feel when we laugh are powerful. Sometimes other emotions are just outside the door knocking to get in on the moment. Have you ever been laughing and then you begin to cry, and the predominant emotion takes over? It's so interesting how closely related these emotions can be, and how good it feels to release them.

When I think about the power of laughter, my mom and dad come to mind right away. They have always had a unique friendship, and as I watched them grow older and life grow more difficult, I saw laughter become the go-to enabler. I mean enabler in a good way. My dad was dyslexic, and back when he was a kid, there wasn't much they could do for that. I know it affected his reading ability, but we experienced other symptoms as well. He lived his life always telling me to go left when he meant right or calling me by my sister's name and vice versa. It was always something we laughed about. As he got older and Parkinson's disease began to overwhelm his body, sometimes it affected his speech. When he talked, it was like he had two marbles rolling around in his mouth. Sometimes he would get frustrated, but mostly he would just laugh. I loved his laugh. It was the most contagious laugh I'd ever heard. Never was there a time when he began to laugh that anyone in the room didn't join in. You couldn't help it. I used to play the movie *Christmas Vacation* every year when we would get together just so I could watch my dad watch it. We all anticipated that perfect moment when Chevy Chase would kick Santa and destroy the reindeer arrangement—and my dad would laugh without making a sound. (Take a breath Dad.) At some point, tears usually appeared. You know the tears that come when your belly and cheeks begin to hurt from all the laughter? I love that feeling. In their later years, my mom would tell me about times when my dad could still drive, and they would go out for their afternoon McDonald's coffee. He would attempt to order "two senior coffees with one cream each," but it was never that easy for him. He would try to get it out and then mess it up, and the absurdity of it all became just too funny. They would laugh and have to pull away and try again later after they regained their composure. Then it became a thing, and every time they approached a drive-thru it turned into a laugh fest. I always loved it when they would tell us their latest story because they would begin to laugh. Again. It wasn't so much about the details, it was about hearing and enjoying their contagious laughter, and then joining in. As times got worse and his ability to take care of himself diminished, life got tough, but they always found something to laugh about. What else could they do? They could have gotten mad, or they could have become bitter and resentful. But, I never saw any of that. They both embraced the positive, and each other.

IF IT'S FUNNY LATER, IT'S FUNNY NOW.

As parents, Mike and I learned the phrase, "If it's funny later, it's funny now." We had to. If you've ever been responsible for a toddler, you know what I mean. You know, the moment you walk in on one of your kids covered in baby powder along with the entire bathroom, and the dog. My first response was always anger because I was thinking about the clean-up. But with three small children, I quickly learned "if it's funny later, it's got to be funny now."

When our oldest daughter Carli was six or seven years old, she was very independent. So independent that one day while we were having lunch at the mall, she asked if she could use the bathroom without me going with her. We were very familiar with the restaurant, and it was pretty empty, so I said "yes." Daddy, on the other hand, wasn't too crazy about the idea, but he said ok. Daddy was right that day. Five minutes went by, then two more, so I went to find out what shenanigans were going on in the bathroom. Much to my surprise, she wasn't there. I began to search the restaurant—no Carli. Finally, I asked the hostess who was standing by the door if she saw a little girl leave. I was terrified when she said "yes." I wondered why she didn't try to stop her, but there wasn't time to ask about that. I was relieved when she said she was alone. The room began to spin and I paused and tried to think like my bold, confident little one. I quickly dashed down the mall walkway, several stores down to the Limited Too where we were headed after lunch to make a return. There she was, barely tall enough to see over the counter, returning her item. The cashier was giving her cash back when I arrived. No one seemed to question this tiny person alone in the mall making a return all by herself. To tell you the truth, after I relaxed from the adrenaline rush, I chuckled to myself at her lack of fear and her ability to handle such an adult task at such a young age. Naturally, I couldn't let her see, and I sternly made sure she knew not to do anything like that again. Daddy agrees the story is funny now that Carli is all grown up and safe, but I believe that it took him several years to see the humor.

Another example of "if it's funny later, it's funny now" is when I was growing up, we went two places for vacation: to my grandpa's cabin in Northern Michigan or to Cedar Point Amusement Park in Ohio. On one trip to Cedar Point, my dad thought it would be funny to have a little fun with my sister. The day had finally arrived; she leaned up against the measuring stick, and sure enough, she was finally tall enough to ride. They climbed into the first car of the roller coaster and were off. My dad, having a little fun at her expense, acted like he was steering the cart. Now this was probably 45 years ago. Back then, the coasters gave you a little ride before they took you up the first hill. So, he tugged and pulled the bar in front of them at every turn, making sure she knew he was steering. That was until they arrived at the top of the first hill. Then without warning, he held up his hands and told her it was her turn to steer, and down the first hill they went. You can imagine her horror. She tugged and pulled on that bar, wide-eyed, all the way around the twists and turns. I'm pretty sure he laughed the entire ride. When they arrived at the end, she had this frozen, freaked-out look of glee on her face, and quite a sense of accomplishment that they all were still alive. I'm not sure how long it took her to figure it out that she didn't actually have to steer the coaster, but I'm pretty sure it took her years before she fully appreciated the humor in it.

Sometimes seeing the humor in a situation is a difficult thing, especially when you are embarrassed. When my kids were young, they would scream for me from all over the house. I was trying to teach them to get up from where they were and look around to try to find me so I didn't always have to stop what I was doing to come to them. This backfired on me in a big way one snowy winter's day. I was on the elliptical in my bedroom watching Regis and Kathy Lee (it was a long time ago). I had a good rhythm going, so when I heard Mallory call my name I didn't yell back at her. I thought if she looked for me at all, she would hear the elliptical and the TV, and find me. They were both pretty loud. She didn't continue to yell my name like usual, so I assumed she had worked out whatever she needed. When I got off the machine a few minutes later, I went downstairs to check on her and Nicholas, and I couldn't find either of them. It had only been about ten minutes since she had called out to me, so I was shocked when I went from room to room searching for them, and they were nowhere to be found. I began to panic. Where could they be? Just as I began to freak out, my phone rang. It was my neighbor Camille who lived a few houses down across the cul-de-sac. "You looking for something?" I couldn't figure out how she knew. "Yes! How did you know?" "I have them." "You have them? How do you have them?" "They came here and told me you left them home alone." Well, I was relieved beyond measure, but then I was embarrassed. What kind of mother was I? I ran to her house in my workout clothes and snow boots, and I can still remember what they looked like when I got there. They were still in their footie pajamas, which were stuffed into their tiny snow boots, and they each had on their little winter coats. Goodness, they were so precious. Mallory was holding Nic's 2-year-old hand and proudly taking care of her little brother. Well, you can imagine how I apologized to Camille and then to my children, and after a good long hug, I stood up and looked at Camille. We both busted out laughing. We decided that it was good that if something really happened at home, Mallory would know who to go to for help.

So now you're probably wondering how many other times I've lost my children. Honestly, I can think of a few other stories I'm sorry to say. Don't judge. Until you've experienced your little one hiding in the clothing rack right beside you in Kohls, you don't know how quickly and easily it can happen. There is humor in my little stories because I have happy endings. I do understand that one slight change in outcome, and these stories would no longer be funny, but tragic. But that's the point. It's that tender line between frustration and relief that makes all the difference. When the room is just a mess but the kid is ok, then it's time to smile. When you discover your kindergartener has more moxie than most 16 year olds, you gotta laugh.

WE WOULD HAVE MADE A GREAT REALITY TV SHOW

I have one more illustration of a "that was funny later, so we need to try to appreciate it now" situation. I hope it gives you a chuckle, or at least makes you smile. Several years ago, when all our kids were still in school, we decided to go on an RV trip out west. I had never been out west or traveled in an RV, so logically I was the person in charge of the trip. (Sarcastic pause.) Well, if you've ever traveled this way, you know that you need to make reservations at RV parks, as they fill up quickly during the summer months. Looking at a map, I booked us a 10-night tour starting in Michigan, heading to Indianapolis, St. Louis, through Kansas to Colorado, down to Moab, Utah and up to Provo, then onto Jackson Hole, Wyoming into Yellowstone National Park, followed by a swing up into Montana to see where Custer last stood. Then we would travel to Devil's Tower and Mt. Rushmore through South Dakota, on to the Windy City and then back home to Michigan. Sounds like a lot, doesn't it? It was—way too much for the length of time we had. Looking back, I'm confident if we had filmed the ordeal—yes, the ordeal—I could have sold it to Ryan Seacrest and made a fortune off the reality TV show.

We began our trip with the unexpected revelation that the air conditioner was broken. It was July. Because our schedule was packed tight, we didn't have time to leave the *RV* at a garage for repair, so we drove the entire time with the windows open. That was fine until we experienced the volume of noise caused by the wind whipping through the cab. We practically had to shout at each other in order to be heard. Not to mention what the wind did to our hair by the end of each day. Good times.

The vehicle I imagined us driving was huge, like the one Robin William's drove in the movie RV, allowing everyone to be together. But the one our budget afforded put the driver and passenger on a lower level, separating them from the rest of the cab. So Mike, the self-designated driver, spent most of the trip missing out on the games and conversations. During arguments and bickering this was a blessing, but mostly it was just a bummer, and not at all what we imagined. Because we had so many miles we had to travel each day, he would wake up early to get us on the road while we all slept, and then he would drive all day. Occasionally, we would make it to a landmark or monument, spend a little time outside of the RV, have a bite to eat, and take a few pictures to document the moment. And I do mean moment, and then we were off again. Remember, we had a schedule to keep and reservations to make, so we had to keep moving. It was all going ok until I got sun poisoning at Arches Park in Moab, Utah. I was so sick during the 200-mile drive from Moab to Provo that I really thought I might die. Once we got to Provo, Mike discovered how sick I really was and took me to the emergency room. I spent the night hooked up to IV fluids and morphine while Mike and the kids slept in the ER parking lot. You're thinking, *This would have made a great reality show.* I know, right?! But wait! There's more! Imagine now how tired everyone was. We were halfway through the trip when we discovered I had missed making a reservation for us while in Yellowstone. We drove from one full RV park to another. There was no room at the inn for us that night. It was around 10 pm when we realized we were out of options and didn't have a place to stay. Now, most people would have just pulled over in a parking lot somewhere, but you need to know my husband to understand why that wasn't an option. We were all so tired and starting to lose it, but he was not going to put us in a situation where a police officer would knock on our door and tell us to move or give us a ticket. No amount of whining and complaining could convince him, and believe me; we were trying. I was willing and eager to take the chance, and I'm pretty sure I didn't hesitate to tell him. Eventually we found an officer and asked her what we should do. She directed us to the amphitheater parking lot on the north side of Yellowstone for the night. For some reason, this set off my sweet, eleven year old, Precious Moment's-faced, go-with-the-flow son Nicholas. He began to cry and grow increasingly agitated. He rarely got upset about anything, so this stopped us all; we were silent. Confused and a little amused, we tried to understand his fear, while he asked us again to please not to go to the amphitheater. We were perplexed and tried to get to the bottom of his issue.

He finally admitted that the amphitheater was where "ladies dance and take their clothes off," and he didn't want us to go there. We tried not to laugh too hard and assured him that it wasn't that kind of "theater" or "club," or whatever place he was imagining. We were able to assure him that where we were going was safe and finally stopped for some much-needed sleep. It should also be noted that we survived the night without any nudity. Actually, we went the whole trip without any nudity, but that's another subject for another day. (Wink!)

I think it was around this time in the trip when we lost Mike's binoculars. You need to understand how much he liked those binoculars to truly appreciate this story. He had saved Cabela's Points from his credit card for I don't know how long. They were way more expensive than he would have ever spent on an item like that, and he loved to use them, especially on this trip where there was so much to see. While packing up to move to the next location, Mike asked the kids to pack everything from the picnic table, including his favorite, expensive binoculars and we quickly pulled away. Well, while we were driving, he wanted to confirm that we packed his binoculars. We began to search and he began to get mad. We searched and searched, and well … you get the point. The further we drove, the angrier he became. For one brief moment, I was spiritual and whispered to the Holy Spirit to show us where they were, but we still couldn't find them. Not until we stopped for lunch, and I got out and walked behind the RV. It was there I spotted them hanging from one of the bicycle handlebars. (Thank you, Holy Spirit!) I stood there in awe, amazed that they had hung on and were undamaged after all the miles we had traveled that day. The family finally noticed that I was frozen, looking in amazement at the RV. They came to see what I was looking at. As soon as Mike saw them, he remembered that he was the one who had put them there. In the chaos of loading up, he had hung them on the bike to ensure they made their way into the RV. They were just swinging back and forth all the way to our next destination and arrived without a scratch. I think Mike ordered humble pie for lunch that day. I wanted to remind him that "if it's funny later, it's funny now," but I thought it best not to say anything at that point.

It was a wild trip, but we made it. For each outrageous story that I've shared, there were three more that I haven't. Somethings are best left undocumented. But for all the crazy stories, what I haven't mentioned are the amazing star-filled nights we witnessed together, and the views of majestic mountains dwarfed by humongous clouds set amidst even bigger skies; or the card games we played for hours; or the white water we rafted in and the horses we rode; or the bonfire we sang around and the BBQ we enjoyed. We climbed on Devil's Tower, witnessed giant presidents made of stone, and marveled at God's sandcastles at the Garden of the Gods. We survived the RV trip from hell, and we did it all together. Along the way, we tried to keep our sense of humor and our perspective.

I share this story because hopefully it's amusing and it made you smile, but also to illustrate the point that life is full of ups and downs; it's rarely all one or the other. This journey called life can get crazy and take some pretty unexpected turns. As you read this, if you are brokenhearted or have been crushed in your spirit, please don't feel like my attempt at humor is not validating your experience. On the contrary, we get to decide if we will allow the Lord to touch that hurting place, or if we will guard it and keep it to ourselves. I know this: when we are hurting, we tend to keep to ourselves, and that's just what the enemy wants. If he can get you isolated and keep you focused on your pain or offense, he's won. Odds are very good that you will not make it out of that dark place alone. But if you surround yourself with people that love God and love you, now you've got the advantage. When times are bad, we get to choose. Choose life, the Bible says, and to me that means choose people. Choose to trust. Choose to believe that God is good and He sees you. Choose laughter, even if it leads to tears.

One woman in the Bible that we may not think of as having a sense of humor is the Proverbs 31 woman. I know many women, even church ladies, get freaked out about this super woman—as she is the goal for most of us. For now, though, let's imagine that she was probably more like us than we know. How many times have you been up in the middle of the night with a sick kid, or put another load of laundry in the washer at 10 pm, or packed lunches for the next day after everyone else is asleep? Perhaps you work late to prepare for a big meeting and stop at parent teacher conferences on your way home. Nobody writes about us in a book, but we do these types of things all of the time. These acts of service and diligence honor God and take care of those we love. Proverbs 31:25 says, *"She is clothed with strength and dignity; she can laugh at the days to come."* Now that's someone I want to hang out with. As a matter of fact, I have a few friends just like that. That's someone I want to be. Why would Solomon feel it is important to say "she laughs at the days to come"? Seems like an interesting thing to point out—kind of out of place with the rest of the text. It speaks to something very important: trust. Trust when you can't see the future. Choosing life. Choosing to believe that what God has said about you and your situation is true. Enjoy the journey and have (the fruit of) joy, even when times are hard, and you don't understand everything.

LAUGHING JESUS

I love the pictures of Jesus where He is laughing. I look forward to the day when we will throw our heads back and bust out laughing together in heaven. I can't relate to the pictures of a sad-faced, skinny Jesus. When I read about what He did and said, I know He was strong and full of life. And His eyes? How beautiful must they be! Eyes that saw the demoniac of the

Gadarenes from across the lake; eyes that looked into the eyes of the woman at the well and spoke life to her; and eyes that took the time to see those who were seemingly insignificant. Matthew, Mark, and Luke all mention the encounter Jesus had with children. Luke 18:15-17 says, *"People were also bringing babies to Jesus to have him touch them. When the disciples saw this, they rebuked them. But Jesus called the children to him and said, 'Let the little children come to me, and do not hinder them, for the kingdom of God belongs to such as these. I tell you the truth, anyone who will not receive the kingdom of God like a little child will never enter it.'"* What an amazing moment that must have been. Can you see it? There is a schedule to keep or some place to go, and Jesus puts it all aside to enjoy these little ones. In this scripture, Jesus took the time to hold the babies and love them. He called the children to Him, held them and blessed them. You know He teased them and kissed them and did what you do with children you love. He also used this opportunity to make a very important point to his disciples. I can imagine Him saying,

> *"Sometimes you just have to release the pressure valve and make room for a little joy to come in."*

"Listen, you serious, religious, well-meaning people. You've got to trust and have faith that I am who I say I am. You've got to love and be open to love, and for heaven's sake, don't forget to play and laugh a little." Isn't that what children do? They aren't guarded or skeptical. They don't hold back laughing, loving, feeling, or crying. If they are told Santa is real, they believe it. Jesus is telling us to believe He is who He says He is—to believe that He is good and that He is the way to the Father. We just need to believe.

If you have found yourself a little too serious these days, maybe taking yourself too seriously, take some time to laugh. May I have permission to say, "You're really not that important? The world will keep spinning if you don't do everything right today." Well, I just did; so too late. (I'm speaking to myself as well.) Take a deep breath and smile. Go ahead, do it. Feels good, doesn't it? Why do you think the bloopers at the end of movies are such a hit? We love to laugh; we love to watch other people laugh. It's good for us—like a strong, effective medicine. We love to watch other people goof because it makes us feel more normal. Misery loves company, and so does messing up. I'm all for setting our standards and goals high and for reaching for the stars. I'm also all for committing your steps and yourself to the Lord in all that you do and working hard to do the absolute best that you can. Sometimes you just have to release the pressure valve and make room for a little joy to come in and embrace the humor that comes from imperfection.

While our kids were growing up, we had a tradition that was always a lot of fun. At the end of a movie, we would head down to the front of the theater and dance to the closing song. Did you know that most theaters have what looks like a dance floor? They do. It's pretty cool. I recall most Disney/Pixar movies end with a fun, upbeat song. The fun drum beat from Mulan comes to mind. So, we would rush down to the front where our make shift dance floor was and dance and be silly as long as the song allowed. We got some strange looks, but for the most part, no one paid attention to what we were doing. It was always fun to dance in an unexpected place. I think it's a good metaphor for life. Take time to dance. Take time to enjoy the people in your life. Take time for God to speak to your heart. He is waiting to dance with you.

What's The Point?

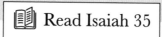

📖 Read Isaiah 35

* What is your main takeaway from this chapter?

* Life is full of ups and downs. It doesn't matter how much money you have, where you live or how famous or not famous you are. We all get sick. We all get rejected. We all feel pain. That's life. Why then do some of us bounce back and move on, while others have a harder time moving forward when difficult trials come our way?

* Social media definitely allows us to enjoy the craziness in life. The videos of toddlers hiding in the corner, marker in hand, creating a master-piece all over their little brother, allows us to see the humor in the moment. Unfortunately, life is not always that simple or that easy. What's your favorite "if it's funny later, it's funny now" story?

* Have you ever danced in an unexpected place?

* Think of the people in your life that make you laugh. The people that are bucket fillers. Life givers. As soon as you are done with this chapter, call them and make a lunch date. It's good medicine.

"The joy of the Lord is your strength."
Nehemiah 8:10

SUGGESTED READING
———————
(Don't have any)
Do something fun with family!

4

Confession:
I'm a People/God Pleaser

"Without faith it is impossible to please God."
Hebrews 11:6

Would you rather please God or trust God? Take a few seconds and really think about it. If you're like me, you might not want to choose one over the other. You may want to answer "both." When I finally gave an honest answer and admitted I wanted to please God first, the reality of that truth changed my life.

Take some time and think about your answer. While you're contemplating that, I would like to address our need to please people. Come on; you know you do it. I know I do. Or at least I did, way more than I would admit. These days, I try not to let other people's opinion sway my choices, but every now and then, I find myself obsessing about what someone said or didn't say, letting it bum me out or steal my joy or even affect my decisions. Just last week I was seriously considering giving up on writing this book. I had written about my church hurt and was considering the potential ramifications. Awake in the middle of the night, I prayed again, "Lord, is this from you? Is this what You want me to do? It's hard Lord. Blah, blah, blah, etc." In the morning, I awoke to a text from a precious friend who knew nothing of my prayer, or this book for that matter. The text consisted of this scripture: 1 Thessalonians 2:4, *"For we speak as messengers approved by God to be entrusted with the Good News. Our purpose is to please God, not people. He alone examines the motives of our hearts"* (NLT). Ah-hem (insert throat clearing sound here). Ok, God. I will concern myself with Your opinion of me. I will obey *Your* voice.

If you would have asked me three or four years ago, on a scale from 1-10 where would I put myself with regards to my concern with what others thought of me, I would have said, maybe 4. I'm a pretty confident person with some pretty strong opinions; however, after living through the past few years, I now realize I was at an 8, maybe 9. Why wouldn't people like me? I'm a pretty good person. Can't they read my mind and know my intentions are good? Nope. Actually, it was pretty egotistical of me to think that most people would like me, and I ask myself now, "Why did I need everyone to like me? Why do I still struggle with wanting everyone to like me?" Was I associating their opinion with God's? I think in many ways, I was. This desire to please has been primary in my life. From my earliest memories, I can remember checking my behavior, trying to be a "good girl" in an effort to please my parents. When I got older, my teachers, my pastors, and even my friends got added to that list, but most of all, my whole life, I've wanted to please God.

THE INTERNET CONNECTION

While we're on the subject of pleasing people, can we take a minute to discuss social media? By now, I'm sure you've felt the adverse effects of comparison on Facebook, Instagram, Twitter, etc. We've all done it at one time or another. It might look like this: taking just a quick peek before going to bed, you see that friend (someone you used to know well, but now is just someone you follow on Facebook) is on vacation—again. She posted a picture of herself in her bathing suit, and you wouldn't be caught dead posting a picture in yours. "If I looked like that, I guess I would too," runs through your mind. You lay your head on your pillow wishing you had more, wishing you were different. Gratitude is out the window as you drift off to sleep with a familiar pain inside that is most definitely not healthy and definitely does not glorify God. Can you relate? Even a little? What's the solution? I'm not sure there is just one, but here are a few simple questions I ask myself to help insure a healthy lifestyle with regard to social media:

- Have you checked your motives lately? How often are you posting? If you find that every time you do something or go somewhere that you think "looks" interesting and you feel the need to post about it, check your intentions. Are you so busy projecting an image that you are neglecting your life?

- How much time do you spend on social media? Time can fly by. If you are checking to see what everyone else is doing or saying several times a day, you may want to set parameters to help you maintain balance. Something meant to be fun can become a huge time stealer.

- If it does not build you up, why are you doing it? Life is too short to spend your time and effort on anything that does not glorify God and pour life into you. I am very picky with my friends. The posts I "like" most are inspiring, honest, and encouraging. All of the other stuff gets deleted, unfriended or ignored.

- Does it inspire gratitude? If you find yourself comparing your life to the lives of others, maybe you need to begin the habit of thanking God for your life every time you pull up that app. Imagine how God feels when you are unhappy with what He has given you and with the people He has placed in your life. An ungrateful heart does not honor God and is not productive for you, at all.

I love to check Facebook and Instagram to keep up with my girls. They are great examples of using social media as a tool to glorify God and honor others. Social media is not the enemy. The devil is the enemy, and don't forget that he comes to steal, kill and destroy. On the contrary, social media is a tool, and with any tool, we can use it to produce something great, or we can use it to be destructive. The choice is yours.

PLEASING VS. TRUSTING

I will step off my soapbox now and get back on topic. Before I got distracted, I was talking about my desire to please people and my overwhelming desire to please God. You might be saying to yourself, "Ok, so what's wrong with that? Doesn't the Bible talk about how we should care about others and be pleasing to God?" Yes, it does. "Doesn't the Word speak of people who desire to please the Father?" Yes, one example of this comes from Jesus himself. John 8:28-29 says this, *"So Jesus said, 'When you have lifted up the Son of Man then you will know that I am the one I claim to be and that I do nothing on my own but speak just what the Father has taught me. The one who sent me is with me; he has not left me alone for I always do what pleases him.'"* So there you go. If Jesus was concerned about the Father being pleased with him, then how much more should we? And aren't we shown a fantastic picture of not only the Trinity but of God being pleased with Jesus in Matthew 3:16-17?

It says, *"As soon as Jesus was baptized he went up out of the water. At that moment heaven was opened and he saw the Spirit of God descending like a dove and alighting on him. And a voice from heaven said, 'This is my Son, whom I love; with him I am well pleased.'"* I love how God made sure Jesus knew He was pleased with him. I think perhaps God made this known more for those around Jesus than for him, but maybe the human side of Jesus was reassured when He received this loving approval from His Father. Having said this, I concede that the desire to please God is scriptural, and in fact, we should desire it. It is His opinion that we should be preoccupied with, not "man's."

I didn't really know how important other people's opinions were to me until I was confronted with people criticizing me openly. I have lived a pretty peaceful life, and I will admit to you that when presented with the question of trusting God vs. pleasing Him, a few years ago, I chose to please Him. I can remember something that happened several years ago that illustrates my mentality about pleasing the Lord. I was struggling with feeling rejected and feeling bad about feeling bad—again. During worship practice for a special service at church, I desperately asked the Lord, "Are You pleased with me?" I think I was afraid that if certain people were not pleased with me, then maybe God wasn't either. The service went on and I forgot about my prayer, but God is so good. He didn't. After service, the guest speaker, who I hold in the highest regard, sought me out and gave me a very nice compliment. He also had an answer from God for me. He said something to this effect, "I just want you to know that I see your humility and your desire to honor the Lord. I think that pleases God." What?! Wow! God used the person I held in highest regard in that room to speak to me about His love for me. I've never had anyone search me out to tell me anything like that before (or since) that day. I love how personal God is. I see His merciful hand reaching down to comfort my hurting heart. But I also see His merciful hand in wanting to address the question that so preoccupied my heart and framed my perspective at that time. I believe He was determined to bring truth and freedom to this issue in my life.

Simply put, this is what God has revealed to me: it is better to trust God than to please Him. For only in trusting Him do I please Him. *"Without faith it is impossible to please God"* (Hebrews 11:6). I know, this is a pretty simple idea, but when you put the wrong one in front of the other, the result can be devastating.

God revealed this simple truth to my husband and me during our time of resting and looking for a new church. He led us to a book called *The Cure* by John Lynch, Bruce McNicol, and Bill Thrall, and used it to begin to change our thinking, to tweak our perspective a few "clicks" as it were.

> *"It is better to trust God than to please Him. For only in trusting Him do I please Him."*

This is what they say about pleasing God vs. trusting Him:

"There's an incredible phrase in Hebrews: "Without faith it is impossible to please God." This statement shows us the path we must take. Only by trusting can we truly please God! If our primary motive is pleasing God, we'll never please Him enough and we'll never learn to trust. Pleasing God is a good desire. It just can't be our primary motivation, or it'll imprison our hearts. If all we bring to God is our moral striving, we're back in the same lie that put us in need of salvation. We're stuck with our independent talents, longing and resolve to make it happen. This self-sufficient effort to assuage a distant deity - it nauseates God. When our primary motive becomes trusting God however, we suddenly discover there is nothing in the world that pleases Him more. Until you trust God, nothing you do will please God. At that point, pleasing God is actually a by-product of trusting God. Pleasing is not a means to our godliness. It is the fruit of our godliness, for it's the fruit of trust. Trusting is the foundation of pleasing God. Lacking that basis of trust is like trying to build a house without a foundation." [3]

Well said, fellas. Here is the take-away in case you missed it. Pleasing God isn't our primary motivation, trusting is. True freedom in serving Jesus puts all of the emphasis on Him, on what He did on the cross. Living life trying to please God as your primary objective puts all of the emphasis and, may I add, all of the pressure on you. The focus is on what you do.

However, when you live your life trusting God as your primary objective, all the pressure is on Him and that, my friend, brings freedom.

Why do you pray? Do you pray because it's what you know you are supposed to do? Do you pray because you hear others talk about how God answered their prayers and you want to experience that too? When you read a book or devotional on prayer or hear a message pertaining to it, are you discouraged and left feeling like a failure (again), or are you motivated and encouraged to pray more? Be honest. If you put the time in to appease a demanding God, you'd better pray a lot. If He's keeping track and demanding more, how much is enough to really please Him? After all, He tells us in 1 Thessalonians 5:17 to *"pray continually."* Better get going, it's on you.

Ok, I'm laying it on a little thick for emphasis, but you get the point. I have had times in my life when I prayed more out of duty than relationship. If you pray because you don't have the answers and you are trusting in The Answer, now the pressure is on Him. When you go to the Giver of life and health when you are in need of healing and strength, then it is up to Him to provide. All you bring to the game is trust and faith. There are times however, (usually daily) when I set aside time to pray. I do this because I have come to understand and experience that prayer changes things. I believe that more today than I ever did before. There are many scriptures that talk about prayer. For us today, I like what Philippians 4:5-7 says about prayer, *"Let your gentleness be evident to all. The Lord is near. Do not be anxious about anything, but in everything, by prayer and petition, with thanksgiving, present your requests to God. And the peace of God, which transcends all understanding, will guard your hearts and minds in Christ Jesus."* Wow. Who doesn't need some of that, everyday? Authentic prayer flows from relationship, not obligation.

Some time ago, I was reading Proverbs 16. My heart was heavy that day. All of my kids were struggling with their specific life issues. If you're a mom, you know that when your children are dealing with issues, those circumstances can weigh on you as well. I feel like verse 3 jumped off the page and kissed me that day. *"Commit to the Lord whatever you do, and your plans will succeed."* I had read that before, but on this day, it was God's roadmap to peace for me. The Hebrew word for commit is galal (gah-lahl), which means

> *"Authentic prayer flows from relationship, not obligation."*

to roll, roll down, roll away. The Bible I was using had a commentary that gave the illustration of a picture of a camel burdened with a heavy load. When the load is to be removed, the camel kneels down, tilts far to one side, and the load rolls off. I love that specific imagery. I was the camel burdened by the heavy load I was carrying. Funny thing is the issues were not even mine; they were my children's. But isn't that the way we are sometimes? When we love people, we are supposed to carry one another's burdens, but these days I find it easier to roll them off on the only One who can do anything about them. He is faithful and true and gracious and good. Why would I hold choose to hold on to my burdens? Psalm 37:5 also speaks this truth, except it comes right out and tells us to trust. *"Commit your way to the Lord, trust also in Him. And He shall bring it to pass."* So now we are back to trust. Why do we pray? Because we trust Him. We rely on Him. We place our life in His hands once again. That is worship.

Here is the prayer I wrote in my notebook that day.

"Today I commit my "work" as a mom to you, Lord. I can no longer bear the burden of the responsibility of my children's choices. And I can no longer carry the anxiety of other people's responses to them. God, I place them again in Your loving, gracious, capable hands. I lean into You, trusting that You will receive this precious load with favor, love and care. This is my prayer today."

THE BOTTOM LINE

Trusting God first = pressure on Him to act. Pleasing God first = pressure on me to perform. The emphasis must change from me to Him. So when you pray, does it please God? Absolutely! It pleases Him because you are placing your trust in Him and placing Him above the issues of life and your own efforts. Pleasing the Father when you pray is the fruit of trusting in Him. It's such a fine line. These two thoughts are so closely related that it almost feels silly to point this out, but when your perspective is fine-tuned and the truth comes into focus, you begin to understand why you are trying so hard. If these two things are out of order, it makes perfect sense why you are exhausted and feel you aren't ever quite measuring up.

This effort to please God first can manifest in any area of your life, not just prayer. Take some time to reflect on the areas in your life where you feel you are not measuring up; better yet, ask the Holy Spirit to reveal to you where you are trusting in your own efforts. Allow Him to make the adjustments to your perspective. It will bring freedom to your life.

I love what they say in *The Cure*: "This life in Christ is not about what I can do to make myself worthy of His acceptance, but about daily trusting what He has done to make me worthy of His acceptance."[4]

This is an issue of identity. Who are we really? When we realize that we are *"a new creature in Christ"* as stated in 2 Corinthians 5:17, we will begin to live from that place instead of striving to get to that place.

The Holy Spirit gave me an illustration regarding this. It's kind of silly, but it really ministers to me. I hope it makes the point to you as well.

PEZ DISPENSER VS. PIÑATA

Living my life trying to please the Lord is like living life with a piñata mentality. When you have a piñata, you may recall that the piñata is held out in front of you, near you. You are blindfolded, so you swing a stick trying to locate it and hopefully hit it hard enough or just right to release the candy inside. I have lived my life knowing that the Lord is close to me. An ever present help in time of need, but He was out there somewhere, and I was constantly seeking Him, working to experience Him— often blindly swinging, trying to please Him with my obedience, service, and my worship. Don't get me wrong; this served me well because by His grace I would often hit the mark, and the "candy"—His wonderful, sweet presence and His love, joy, mercy and truth—would come flowing out. And it was awesome! He was in my life for sure, but much like with a piñata, there was usually a striving to obtain. I did know that the Holy Spirit lived inside me. That He came to reside in me at salvation. I understood that. I just didn't always live like it.

Now I understand that I am more like a Pez dispenser. You know, one of those candy holders shaped like different cartoon or movie characters. When you pull the head back, out pops a candy. Let me explain. When 1 John 4:4 says, *"The one who is in you is greater than the one who is in the world,"* it means I am to live from Him not for Him. 1 John 7:38 says, *"Whoever believes in me, as the Scripture has said, streams of living water will flow from within him."* I am a carrier of His presence. His sweet Spirit is the "candy", the fruit, the sweet reward in the dispenser. I knew that; I just wasn't responding to life like it. Even though there are times in life when I must seek the Lord and seek His face, He is with me. He abides in me, never to leave me. Acts 6:8 says, *"Stephen, a man full of God's grace and power, did great wonders and miraculous signs among the people.*" How did he do this? The "sweet" presence and power of the Holy Spirit was in him, flowing through him. All he had to "do" was allow the Holy Spirit to do the work through him. That's a heck of a lot easier than trying to get the Lord to do something by using me.

Stop swinging. Stop trying. Stop waiting.

Take a deep breath and allow the Holy Spirit of God who dwells in you to speak to you, to propel you, to minister through you. Begin to live from Him instead of for Him. It takes all the pressure off.

Study Guide

What's The Point?

 Read Hebrews 11

* What is your main takeaway from this chapter?

* Priorities are important, aren't they? You can have several really good things in front of you, but if your priorities are out of order, your life can get out of order. If you put your children before your marriage, your marriage will be weak. If you put your spouse before the Lord, your life will be difficult. Hobbies before job… Job before family… You get it. All good things, but in the wrong order, good things can reap bad fruit.

* What is your priority? To trust God or to please Him? What are you trusting God for today?

* I've been saved for over forty years, and I'm still learning what it is to live like a daughter instead of an orphan/slave. Slaves live with a piñata mentality. Gotta do more. Gotta be better.

Daughter's trust daddy to take care of them. They have a key to the house. They know who they are and whose they are. Is there an area of your life where you tend to live more like a slave than a daughter?

* What are you afraid of? What are you insecure about?

* Ask the Holy Spirit to give you wisdom and revelation regarding these areas in your life. Remember, the Holy Spirit lives in you. He is your Helper and Comforter. Don't ignore Him.

"Trust in the Lord with all of your heart and lean not to your own understanding; in all your ways acknowledge him, and he will make your paths straight."
Proverbs 3:5

SUGGESTED READING

The Cure by Bill Thrall, Bruce McNicol and John Lynch

5

Confession:
I've Lived Most of My Life Afraid

*"There is no fear in love. But perfect love drives out fear,
because fear has to do with punishment. The one who fears
is not made perfect in love."*
1 John 4:18

I've heard it said, the most important thing a man
thinks about, is what he thinks, when he thinks
about God. (Selah) You may want to pause and
think about that. I agree. What you think about when
you think about God is the lens through which you
judge every experience. Do you think He is distant and
angry? Do you think about how tender and present He
is? Do you view Him more as Judge than Father, and if
you do, is He fair and good or is He harsh and unfair?
If you have had a difficult relationship with your earth-

ly father or other authority figures, you may easily see through a lens that sees God as harsh and condemning. But if you're like me, it's not that simple. It's more a mixture of the two. He is loving Father and the Judge of all men—a jealous God, the Creator of the universe, my Provider, the Alpha and Omega, a compassionate and gracious God, the Sovereign One, the lover of my soul, a Consuming Fire, etc. All of these descriptions are accurate, and yet some seem to contradict others. If we don't look at the whole Word of God to establish a complete picture of who God really is, our lens of "truth" will be out of focus. So here we are again, back in the eye doctor's chair needing the Great Physician to make another adjustment.

I went to high school and college in the 80s. We danced to Michael Jackson, Kenny Loggins, and Journey, styled our hair big and cut our sweat shirts to dangle off our shoulders, Flash Dance style. We watched Tom Cruise fly jets, laughed when Harry Met Sally and held our breath every Friday the 13th because we were afraid Jason would find us and chase us down the street, axe in hand. I don't know why, but when I was in high school, I enjoyed watching scary movies. When everyone else was genuinely afraid, I would laugh. The more ridiculous the scenario, the more I enjoyed it. Looking back, I know it's out of character for me. I must have been drawn to the thrill of it. Maybe because I was cautious in real life, I found it a fun escape. Who knows? But I distinctly remember driving my girlfriends home after one of those ridiculous movies and having to walk them to their door because they were so afraid. I, however, could walk alone and be alone without any problem. For some reason, those movies never got to me. Now that I'm an old church lady, I know how foolish it was to watch those movies because I could have opened myself up to a spirit of fear. Chalk it up to youthful stupidity.

Thankfully, though, I've never had much of a problem with fear. So why did I title this chapter "I've Lived Most of My Life Afraid"? Hang on; I'm getting there. I don't struggle with the same everyday fears that many others do. I leave my doors unlocked, love to speak in public and will be the first person to go on a moonlight walk on the beach with you. Some of the things in life that scare people the most don't bother me. I have struggled with a different kind of fear—the fear of being out of the will of God. From sermons about the Lord's "umbrella" of protection, I have learned through the years about the dangers of being out of God's will. I certainly never wanted to step out from beneath it. However, when Paul says, *"Therefore, do not be foolish, but understand what the Lord's will is"* (Ephesians 5:17), I'm not sure I understood what he was communicating. My

"I have always been afraid of being out of the will of God."

understanding of the topic was a little off, at least a click or two. I have lived most of my life surrendered to the Lord's will, praying to know and understand

His perfect will for my life, for my day. But I was living from a place of fear, with an orphan mentality. I doubted God's goodness and my ability to hear the Spirit speak, so I would wait and pray, pray and wait, and unfortunately, not much got done because I lived life afraid.

STEPPING OUT

Many years ago, I felt the desire to record a CD. I found myself day dreaming about what kind of music I would create. Hearing a song, I would think about how fun it would be to record it with the style of music I liked. I would pray about it and ask God if it was ok for me to pursue it. Years went by. I'm not exaggerating; years went by. The desire never went away; as a matter of fact, it only increased. When praying, the idea would come to mind, and I would ask the Lord again if it was from Him or of my flesh—a need for fame or some kind of validation? (I understand now that much of this second guessing was a byproduct of the culture of the church I was in at the time. There wasn't a lot of freedom to fail or take a risk.) I never heard a specific answer, and a record producer never walked through the doors of our church and proclaimed it was time for me to make a record. So I didn't. After years of seeking, the Lord used a message from a visiting pastor to speak to me. Simply put, I heard in my spirit, in an almost irritated voice, "Why wouldn't I want you to make music that glorifies Me?" The question almost seems too simple to be God, doesn't it? But wait ... isn't that exactly what I'm learning? Religion makes things difficult. The devil makes things complicated. Jesus says, "Come to me as a little child." The cool thing is, I shared with the visiting pastor how the Lord had spoken to me during his message. He proceeded to hook me up with a very talented producer, one who would work for free because he was looking for experience, and also knew musicians that were way more talented than I am. God opened the door, and all I had to do was walk through it. Why was I so afraid? It must have been what I was thinking about when I thought about God's will.

A few years ago, I heard a message by Pastor Steven Furtick from Elevation Church in Charlotte, North Carolina called "God's Will is Whatever." This message masterfully talks about God's sovereign will for mankind, His ways, and His personal will for my life. This teaching, along with a few others, was the beginning of me no longer living life afraid. The title of the message comes from Colossians 3:17, which says, *"And whatever you do, whether in word or deed, do it all in the name of the Lord Jesus, giving thanks to God the Father through him."*

I used to live my life from a paused or stationary position, moving only when directed by God. As I mentioned before, living with this perspective causes you to potentially miss what God has for you to accomplish. This outlook stems from a pleasing God mentality and is motivated by fear. If I am to please

Him, then I must be careful to do only what He is specifically telling me. What happens if I'm wrong? What happens if I thought I heard Him speak, but He really didn't? Hello! No wonder it took me five years to start making a CD.

Here is the shift that has occurred in my life: I now live from a place of motion, continually being led by the Spirit of God that lives inside me. I am trusting that if I take a step in the wrong direction, God can and will lovingly guide me back to where I belong. He is gracious, slow to anger and abounding in love. I am His, and He is for me, not against me. The devil is against me and wants me to be paralyzed by fear, and if he can use a distorted fear of God to keep me inactive, that's just fine with him. The devil doesn't need me to be afraid of him specifically. His goal is for me to be ineffective for Christ. Period.

Sometimes finding the will of God is as simple as asking the question, "What do I want to do?" I find in my life that the Lord leads me by divine pushes or desires. With the example of making the CD, I had a "want to" that wouldn't go away. What I could have done was pray about it, asking the Lord for direction, and then if I still felt a divine pull to it, I could have started to step out in faith. If all doors were closed and it was difficult to get things started, I could have re-evaluated my decision. The Lord has always provided for what He has called me to do. His provision is confirmation to me that I am in His will. Don't get me wrong, the process was not without effort, struggle and much patience. But there was a divine provision and anointing all along the way.

GET IN POSITION TO HEAR

So, how do you hear from God? There are many things I've placed in my life to position myself to hear. These disciplines turn on the radio of my heart and mind to pick up the frequency of His voice, so to speak. For me, the habits of reading the Word, praying, surrounding myself with other people that hear His voice and life situations are key.

- **The Word of God:** King David says in Psalm 119:89, 103, 105 - *"Your Word, O Lord, is eternal; it stands firm in the heavens. How sweet are your Words to my taste, sweeter than honey to my mouth! Your Word is a lamp to my feet and a light for my path."* The Word of God is our comprehensive authority. Many decisions we make in life are not specifically addressed in the Bible (Should I have another child? Should I take that job offer? Should I join the worship team at church?). However, God's Word and His principles apply to all areas of life. How can you judge your choices by the Word of God if you are not in the Word of God? The first fundamental choice we make to know the character and nature of God and the person of Jesus is to read and study the Bible. Disciplined, daily reading will keep you in the center of God's will more than any other thing. Please indulge me, though; I must add this request. Don't get religious and stressed-out about it. Everyone receives and learns differently. I used to try to read through the Bible once every year like others I knew, and even though I read almost every day, I was so rushed that I hardly got anything out of it. Once I started taking my time, taking notes in a journal where I could document what the Lord was saying to me, with the ability to get creative with quotes, pictures and prayers, the Word came alive. When I was checking off a box on a list, I felt bad when I missed a day. When I began meeting with the Giver of life and breath, I was bummed when I missed a day.

Several years ago when my daughter Carli was heading off to Sydney to live I had been praying about the situation. The Lord spoke to me during my daily reading in Isaiah 43:1-3. He brought peace to my soul and reassured me that she is His daughter and He will take care of her. It says, *"But now, this is what the Lord says – he who created you, O Jacob, he who formed you, O Isreal; "Fear not, for I have redeemed you; I have summoned you by name; you are mine. When you pass through the waters, I will be with you; and when you pass through the rivers, they will not sweep over you. When you walk through the fire, you will not be burned; the flames will not set you ablaze. For I am the Lord, your God, the Holy One of Israel, your Savior; I give you Egypt for your ransom, I give Cush and Seba in your stead."*

- **The Holy Spirit/Prayer:** You may know Him as a still small voice or a gentle whisper. During times of prayer and waiting in the Lord's presence, He speaks. You may hear words in your mind or you may experience a "knowing" in your heart. You may experience Him lifting the words off a page kissing your understanding or you may get a 2x4 upside the head from Him while listening to a message at church. I have found the more I recognize and trust that I've heard His voice and leading, the easier it is to recognize His voice and leading. In Acts 20:22 Paul says that he was *"compelled by the Spirit to go to Jerusalem."* How did the Spirit compel him? It doesn't say, but I can tell you how the Holy Spirit compelled me to do something that saved my son's life. I was 39 weeks pregnant and anxious to get my ankles back, among other things. One morning I woke up with what I can only call a holy determination to deliver. "It just so happened" that I had my weekly appointment with my doctor that morning. At the time, I did not recognize this push, pardon the pun, as being from the Holy Spirit, but I did not ignore the motivation either. Once in the office, I made my case to the doctor that "today was the day." I implored him to meet me at the hospital and break my water to induce labor. I still had a little time to go, so imagine my surprise when he agreed. I will spare you the details, but I will tell you that there were no indications as to anything being high risk or questionable through the whole pregnancy.

Once in labor, I had to lay on one side because my son's heartbeat was affected when I moved to my other side, but no one seemed concerned about this. When I finally delivered my son, the cord was wrapped around his neck, and there were two knots in his cord. The doctor had no idea about either, as indicated by his surprise when my son's head came out with the cord pulling tight on his airway. He was shocked at first but then sprang into action, his training and experience took over, and my son was born healthy and beautiful. Later that evening, the doctor came and sat down at my bedside and asked me what motivated me to convince him to induce me. I think even he was surprised that he agreed. He told me, "if I had waited one more day, I would have delivered a dead baby." I apologize for being so blunt, but those words, 19 years later, still give me a sick feeling when I think about that moment. Was there a scripture involved? Not this time. Did I hear a warning from a still small voice? Nope. Just a divine push, a compelling that I allowed to move me. Thank you, Holy Spirit. Nicholas has been a precious gift to my life. He is a pleasure and a joy. This fall he headed off to college, thus completing the emptying of my nest. My, how time flies.

Before leaving this topic, I would like to mention the baptism of the Holy Spirit. I personally pray "in the Spirit and with my understanding." Many times when I am confronted with a situation where

I don't know what to do or say or even pray, I pray in tongues. Luke says this in Acts 2:4, *"All of them were filled with the Holy Spirit and began to speak in other tongues as the Spirit enabled them."* And again in Acts 8:15-17, *"When they arrived, they prayed for them that they might receive the Holy Spirit, because the Holy Spirit had not yet come upon any of them: they had simply been baptized into the name of the Lord Jesus. Then Peter and John placed their hands on them, and they received the Holy Spirit."* And if you recall, Paul prayed in the Spirit too. In 1 Corinthians 14:15 he says, *"I will pray with my spirit, but I will also pray with my mind; I will sing with my spirit, but I will also sing with my mind."* And in verse 18 he goes on to say, *"I thank God that I speak in tongues more than all of you."* It is my experience that praying and singing in the spirit brings godly insight to my mind and peace to my soul. Please indulge me in adding a note here: don't be weird. It doesn't have to get weird just because it's spiritual and maybe a little mysterious. I don't pray louder or moan or make a spectacle of myself. I cringe when someone is causing a commotion and drawing attention to themselves. I would say that 80% of the time that I pray or sing in the Spirit, I am alone in my car or my home. I tell you that because it's for me, not for others to hear. If you have decided that this is not for you because you've seen people get weird, may I urge you to ask the Lord if the baptism of the Holy Spirit is for you? I challenge you to pray about it. Take some time to study what the Bible has to say about it. Talk to a respected leader about it. If you are looking to go deeper on this issue, Joyce Meyer, one of the most normal, highly respected speakers around, has some great teaching on the subject. If you want to dig really deep, check out what Jack Hayford has to say on the topic.

- **People:** God uses people to bring wisdom, guidance and council to our lives. Proverbs 11:14 (MSG) says this, *"Without good direction the people lose their way, the more wise council you follow the better your chances."* I'm blessed to say that I have 'people.' If you don't have what you would call 'your people,' ask God for some and then go find you some. We were not meant to do life alone. If I am looking for direction regarding a financial decision, I go to a person who is generous and has managed their money well. I don't go to a person, no matter their title or influence, who is always struggling to pay their bills. If I am confused about a problem with my marriage, I trust a faithful friend who still likes their spouse and has been through some trials to give me advice. God speaks to me often through my pastor and other ministers of the gospel. He speaks to me through music and lyrics that people write and create. God can even use your critics to speak wisdom into your life. Sometimes when "haters gonna hate," we need to pay attention to what they are saying. Judge the message they are bringing, ask God to reveal any truth that needs to be adopted and throw the rest away—for good! A godly friend is a treasure. I'm happy to say that I have a wonderful group of very mature, trusted friends that speak into my life often. Most of the time, they bring a word of encouragement to me, but other times they have my permission to bring a word of correction to my life. We don't always see the poppy seed in our teeth, the toilet paper stuck to our shoe or the disrespectful tone in our voice. I say, bring it on! I want to know. I want to grow. Proverbs 27:17, written by the wisest man to ever live says, *"As iron sharpens iron, so one person sharpens another."* If you don't have a trusted friend or mentor in your life that can speak the truth to you at all times, ask God for one. Our closest friends came into our lives a few months after I prayed and asked God for a fun, spiritually mature couple to "do life" with.

Jesus had people. He placed obvious value on Peter, James, John and the rest of the disciples. If you have a tribe you are doing life with, thank the Lord. They are a precious gift! If you don't, ask God to lead you to like-minded people and then join a small group or volunteer. If you are friendly and open, you may be surprised at the response you get from others.

- **Life Situations:** This can be a biggie. Let's face it, desperation causes us to look to God. King David wrote most of the book of Psalms and much of his writings were inspired because he was running for his life. In Psalm 34:17 he says, *"The righteous cry out, and the Lord hears them; he delivers them from all their troubles. The Lord is close to the brokenhearted and saves those who are crushed in spirit. A righteous man may have many troubles, but the Lord delivers him from them all; he protects all his bones, not one of them will be broken."* Several years ago my husband and I went through 13 months of unemployment. Those months were hard. The months following those months were hard. We were challenged. Did we really trust God with our lives? Did we really trust Him as our Provider? Were we going to remain a team or were we going to get stressed and let the enemy into our

"Great revelation and growth occur during times of great trials."

home? Dependency and desperation brought us closer to the Lord and to one another. Because of the time availability of not working, we spent more time seeking God together as a couple and individually. The Lord ministered His amazing grace, love and faith to both of us. We wouldn't trade the money that was lost for what God did in and through us during that time. After that experience, I decided I wanted to live desperately every day. Desperate for God's presence and voice in my life. Desperate for His provision and miraculous power to be displayed in my life. Desperate for His love to fill me so that it can overflow out of me. If you are going through a painful trial, don't despair. You are not alone. God sees you and He is waiting to speak to you. He longs to pour out His love and grace on you. Fix your eyes on Jesus. Press into Him and allow Him to do His work in you. Great revelation and growth occur during times of great trials.

GET IN GEAR

So, where are you today? Are you in park, living life from a stationary place of fear and timidity, or are you in drive, moving and walking daily, trusting in the Holy Spirit who lives inside of you and the Word of God to lead you wherever you need to go?

If you blow it, and you will, is God not able to get you where you need to be? Romans 8:28 reminds us, *"And we know that in all things God works for the good of those who love him, who have been called according to his purpose."* Remember, perfect love casts out fear, and God is love. If you've been waiting to take that step of faith, don't let fear paralyze you. Perhaps it's time to pray for direction, get into the Word and ask those around you for advice. If you don't get a "no" or a caution signal in your spirit, start walking in the direction of your dreams. God will guide you. Trust Him.

Study Guide

What's The Point?

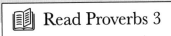

📖 Read Proverbs 3

* What is your main takeaway from this chapter?

* First things first. Before God can make our path straight, we must acknowledge Him as our God and surrender our life to His will. If we are seeking wisdom that is from Him, it makes being in and staying in His will so much easier. He is sovereign and does work all things together for our good, but we absolutely have a part to play in what we do and where we end up.

* What do you think when you think about God?

* Do you question His goodness? If your answer is yes, ask the Lord to reveal to you what or who in your life impacted how you see your heavenly Father. Allow Him to speak truth to that wound or situation.

* If you knew you couldn't fail, what is the one thing you would do?

* Now think about why you're not doing it. Are you afraid of failure? Will you be embarrassed if you make a mistake or it doesn't work out? Boy, I've lived a lot of my life that way. When you look at the inventors, business moguls or anyone really successful at what they do, there is one common denominator: they have all failed at one time or another. They have learned from it and moved on. Heck, I've said to myself, "What if no one buys or reads my book?" Then I remind myself that the process of writing is what has brought so much of my healing. So, whether my book is on the New York Times Best Seller list (Yes! Let's go with that) or only my close friends and family read it, it's not a waste of time and effort, and I won't be embarrassed because I tried. I obeyed.

* What is keeping you from stepping out? What is the worst thing that could happen?

* People will tell you that you shouldn't try, and the circumstances may not be perfect, but what if you started to do that thing God placed in your heart/mind to do? What if you did succeed? Wouldn't that be fun?!

"But Jesus immediately said to them: 'Take courage! It is I. Don't be afraid.' 'Lord, if it's you,' Peter replied, 'tell me to come to you on the water.' 'Come,' He said. Then Peter got down out of the boat, walked on the water and came to Jesus." Matthew 14:27-29

SUGGESTED READING

God is Good by Bill Johnson

6

Confession:
I'm Addicted to His Presence ...
and Diet Coke®

"Blessed are those who have learned to acclaim you, who walk in the light of your presence, O Lord."
Psalm 89:15

At this point, I need to pause and declare to you how wonderful I know God to be. Take a minute to agree with me that God is good! He is faithful and He is the perfection of love. He has given us Jesus, the only One in whom we find salvation. Jesus is worthy of our praise. Philippians 2:9 tells us, *"God highly exalted Him, and granted to Him the name above every other name."* In verse 11, we are told that it is *"to the glory of God the Father"* when we declare that Jesus is our Lord and He is king. It pleases God. Let's take a moment to lift up the name of Jesus together right now. He is above every situation, every disease, every broken heart, and shattered dream. Jesus is the name we call when we are lonely and in need because in Jesus there is healing, life, peace, hope, joy, and so much more. May I confess to you that I want to know Him more? I am desperate for His presence in my life. I have spent a lot of time getting to know more about Jesus. Today I just want to know Him, and I have found that the more I know Him, the more I want to know Him. As I write this, my words seem so inadequate to express what I know to be true. Yet as I fumble awkwardly trying to bring Him glory with my limited vocabulary and limited understanding, He is faithful to be near. I sense His presence in my life. It is my prayer as you read these words and agree with me in your spirit, you sense His presence too. This I know, God cannot resist our worship. John 4:23 tells us He is looking for it. *"Yet a time is coming and has now come when the true worshipers will worship the Father in spirit and truth, for they are the kind of worshipers the Father seeks."* Let's not wait for Sunday to give Him praise. He is waiting for you.

I'm thankful that God is faithful to manifest His wonderful presence no matter where I am. Whether I am singing a new song to Him in my car or I break into dance singing along with Israel Houghton in my kitchen, He is there. When I am on my knees in the darkness of night, He is there. Sometimes I sense His presence and other times I don't, but I trust that He sees me and hears me whether I feel Him or not.

However, as much as I enjoy alone time with the Lord, I must confess, there is nothing on earth like when I get together with other believers and we corporately declare who we serve together. When we rejoice in His faithfulness together. When we bask in His love together. When we are still in the silence of His presence together. That is one of my favorite things. I'm addicted to it. One of my all-time favorite songs is "Holy Ground" by Geron Davis and Tim Pedigo because it declares this truth so nicely. It was sung at my wedding almost 30 years ago and again at my Dad's memorial just a few years ago. It goes like this...

"As I walked through the door, I sensed His presence.
And I knew this was a place where love abounds.
For this is His temple, Jehovah God abides here,
And we are standing in His presence on holy ground.

We are standing, on holy ground.
And I know that there are angels all around.
Let us praise Jesus now.
We are standing in His presence on holy ground.

In His presence there is joy beyond measure.
And at His feet peace of mind can still be found.
If you have a need I know He has the answer.
Reach out and take it for you are standing on holy ground." [5]

If you look this song up, the versions you will hear will most likely be dated. It's very 80s, but the words continue to be true no matter the style of music in which they are sung. I guess that's why I love going to church, or small group, or even lunch with friends. I am anticipating those moments in His presence that we can only get when we are together.

CHOOSE LIFE

I am addicted to His presence, and although I experience the Holy Spirit the most during times of worship, praise and prayer, I know that is just the beginning. I also sense Him in the everyday-ness of life. Don't get me wrong; there are times when I find myself at home alone and I feel sad and lonely. There are times I am frustrated with life not meeting my expectations and I am faced with the reality of today. There are times when life just gets hard and the people I love are hurting, so I hurt too. But it is in those times of loneliness and pain that I encourage myself in the Lord, much like David must have done, and I remind myself that God's plans for my life are good, and He will never leave me or turn away from me. This is when I am presented with the choice to choose life and not hold on to the death that wants to get a hold of my heart. Each time I make this decision, it is like sending an invitation to the Holy Spirit to do what only He can do. My pain may not go away right away, and sometimes it takes me longer than others to make this choice, but when I do, I have a Comforter who is with me, ready and waiting to do what only He can do.

Recently I found myself getting frustrated during a time of worship at our church. It was the bridge of the third song, we were declaring the greatness of our God, and I was absolutely enjoying myself, eyes closed. When I opened my eyes, I was taken back by the amount of people in the congregation who appeared not to be worshiping. Now, I understand that everyone is different. Some people like to hoot and holler and others like to remain still out of reverence. I know this. But the Spirit of God was absolutely moving in that place, and anyone who wanted to get in on it could have. So why were so many people seemingly not entering in? This was the topic of my prayer that night as I went to sleep. As a worship leader, I am always evaluating what we are doing, how we are doing it, and most importantly, why we are doing it. Honestly, I was expecting to get an answer from the Lord about the need to simplify the music or teach more about worship during the set. A day or two later, I was listening to a podcast (I'm not sure who it was), and the pastor started talking about worship, which was interesting because that was not the topic of his message. Anyway, he said something that shouted the answer to my prayer. He made the statement that the reason people do not surrender in worship on Sunday is that they do not live surrendered to Him the rest of the week. Yes! That was it! It was an issue of surrender.

For most of my life, I have been able to walk into an atmosphere of worship and jump right in. With the first song or prayer, boom I'm in. I don't usually need time to "warm up" because there is an attitude and a reality of His presence in my life daily. Now, you may read that and say to yourself, "Geesh, who does she think she is?" I know I'm nobody special, but let me tell you why I can make this bold statement: it's not about me. It's always about Jesus. I know I need Him, desperately, every moment of every day. He has called me by name, and I have surrendered to His love for me; I have experienced it. I am aware of it every single day. So, when I get to join in with others to petition Him for strength or to thank Him for His goodness, I'm ready because I'm so aware of my need for those things in my life. I am continually yielding to His will for my life because I understand left to myself I will live selfishly and foolishly. So, I enter in quickly because I understand my place. It is bowing before His throne daily, sometimes hourly because of my great need for Him. It's not about me. It's all about Jesus.

MAKE THE SHIFT

Do you find it uncomfortable to lift your hands in worship? That's a pretty common thing, especially if you weren't raised in a church where it was a regular part of worship. When I talk to people who have struggled with displaying their worship outwardly, they are usually pleasantly surprised after they step out and raise their hands, bend a knee or add words of adoration that aren't in the lyrics of the song. When they finally get the courage to step out of their comfort zone and take their worship to a new level, they realize no one else was paying any attention to them. No bell went off or spotlight found them. Whatever they thought would happen when they stepped out and made this bold gesture, didn't happen. That's when they realize that it's not about them; it's about the One they are worshiping. Discovering this brings freedom and true worship. How can we worship God when we are preoccupied with ourselves? It's just not possible. I realize the ability to shift focus from ourselves to Him is a process, a growing and learning process, but it can become second or hopefully even first nature. The habit of yielding to the Lord, of focusing on and seeking Him as situations arise throughout the day is what I'm talking about. How do you begin to do that? How do you begin to become aware of His presence in your life? You surrender. First, you understand that at salvation your life is no longer your own. Second, you invite the Holy Spirit, who lives in you (if you have accepted Jesus as your Savior), to have His way in your life. You invite Him to speak to you and guide you. The Holy Spirit is waiting to lead you and direct you. If your thoughts and ideas, talents, time and choices are surrendered to Him, then you become a vessel for His presence to flow through. You have the choice to be available and to trust that He is good and that He won't take you anywhere that is not good for you. If you don't trust Him, you can't surrender to Him. Or let me say it this way, you will only be able to surrender to Him as much as you trust Him.

"Oceans," Hillsong United
"Spirit lead me where my trust is without borders,
Let me walk upon the waters, wherever You would call me.
Take me deeper than my feet could ever wander
And my faith will be made stronger
In the presence of my Savior." [6]

Romans 15:13 says, *"May the God of hope fill you with all joy and peace as you trust in Him, so that you may overflow with hope by the power of the Holy Spirit."* Proverbs 3:5 says, *"Trust in the Lord with all of your heart and lean not on your own understanding; in all your ways acknowledge Him, and He will make your paths straight."*

We read those amazing words, and thousands of other scriptures, and sometimes we can be left knowing that the Word is true, but not knowing exactly how to make it a reality in our daily lives. We say, "Yes, Lord" when we read it, and then we go on about our day hoping we can do it.

HOW'S YOUR HEART?

Before I begin this portion of the chapter, I must preface what I am about to say. In Romans 8:9 it says, *"You, however, are controlled not by the sinful nature but by the Spirit, if the Spirit lives in you."* And then in Romans 8:11 Paul goes on to write, *"If the Spirit of Him who raised Jesus from the dead is living in you, He who raised Christ from the dead will also give life to your mortal bodies through his Spirit, who lives in you."* I want to be clear, when we become a follower of Christ, the Spirit of God lives inside of us. We are born again in our spirit. Behavior, good or bad doesn't change this. As you continue to read, you will understand why I am making this distinction now. I just want to make sure that when I speak of God's presence in our life, I am speaking about a greater level of anointing, awareness, favor, etc., not our salvation.

I am far from a Bible scholar, and the last thing I want to do is to give you a list of things to do to be more aware of His presence in your life; however, the Bible does give us direction, and it would be foolish to pray for a move of the Spirit of God to transform us while ignoring what the Word says about it. There is so much I could say, so many directions I could go, but I feel the Lord wants me to ask you, "How's your heart?"

Better yet, take a moment and ask the Holy Spirit, "How is my heart?" When we judge ourselves, we either tend to be generous and go easy on ourselves, or we are overly critical. I know that's how I can be. Take a moment and let Him speak to you.

Come on; you can wait longer than that. "Lord, what do you want to say to me about my heart?" Be still and give Him a chance to speak.

Paul tells the Ephesians in 4:17, *"I tell you this, and insist on it in the Lord, that you no longer live as the Gentiles do, in the futility of their thinking."* And in verse 18 it says, *"They are darkened in their understanding and separated from the life of God because of the ignorance that is in them due to the hardening of their hearts."*

Paul tells us the problem was two-fold: wrong thinking and a hard heart. It's interesting how they go together. If you doubt that God's thoughts toward you are good, that He is full of love for you no matter your circumstances, and that He is able to work all things together for your good, then you may someday find yourself with a hard or bitter heart.

So, if you're not addicted to His presence or even aware of it daily, but you want to be, may I recommend you do a heart check? Our heart is precious and delicate. We are told to guard and protect it, so I think it is safe to say that a healthy heart will bring a greater awareness of the Holy Spirit in your life. For our discussion, I would like to offer three attributes of a healthy heart: gratitude, obedience and love.

A GRATEFUL HEART

Let's begin by taking a look at King David, a man after God's own heart. In Psalm 118:28-29 he says this, *"You are my God, and I will give you thanks; you are my God, and I will exalt you. Give thanks to the Lord, for he is good; his love endures forever."* Notice what he thinks about when he thinks about God. In Psalm 136:1 he says, *"Give thanks to the Lord, for he is good. His love endures forever."* David definitely enjoyed the Lord's presence in his life because he knew Him, and he believed in his heart that the Lord was good. In response to this belief, he had a lifestyle of gratitude and worship. David continually voiced his trust in God and enjoyed His presence whether he was singing with his harp, working in the field tending his sheep or even running for his life.

In Colossians 3:15 Paul writes, *"Let the peace of Christ rule in your hearts, since as members of one body you were called to peace. And be thankful."* It's kind of funny; he talks about living a peaceful life then adds be thankful. The way it is written, it sounds like he thought for a minute about how to live at peace and added the statement "be thankful." If Paul could speak to us today, I can imagine he would say something like this, "Would you knock off the complaining people and grow up!? Christ has paid an amazing price so we could live an abundant, overcoming life. Let's focus on what we have and be grateful for it so we can give this amazing gift of salvation to a lost and dying world."

In Luke 17 we are told about 10 lepers who were healed by Jesus. The story not only shows that Jesus has the authority to heal, but it also shows the importance of gratitude. One of the lepers *"came back, praising God in a loud voice. He threw himself at Jesus' feet and thanked him. Jesus asked, 'Were not all ten cleansed? Where are the other nine? Was no one found to return and give praise to God except this foreigner?'"* (He wasn't from where they were from). Only 1 out of 10 had a grateful heart. I wonder if those would still be the odds today? Would anyone go back? Would I? Would you? I wonder.

How do you think it makes God feel when we live life with a chip on our shoulder? When we act like He hasn't done anything for us and does not care? When we live in constant fear? "I wish I had a bigger/nicer house; I wish I had a different job; I wish my husband would...; if only my child would..., etc." If we have come to know Him personally through the salvation He provided on the cross, isn't that enough to live with a grateful heart!? Let me answer for us: Yes! In the past, when my children have been ungrateful, not only did it hurt my heart, but it also didn't make me want to give them more. It made me want to grab the ice cream cone out of their hand and give it to the dog. I may have done that now that I think back. So, here are some questions for you:

- How many times a day do you complain?

- When was the last time you paid attention to what was coming out of your mouth?

- When something goes wrong, what is your first response?

Often we develop habits over time that we aren't aware of. Sometimes we partner with the devil and don't even know we're doing it. If this is something that you struggle with, and we all do on some level, ask the Lord to reveal it to you. He can help you trade that bad habit for a godly one. I pray that as you read this, you will be overwhelmed by the love of God. I pray that His grace and mercy will become a reality in your life, and His great love for you will change your perspective and transform your mind so that you will be more grateful in your spirit.

Perhaps you find yourself in the doctor's chair (remember the eye doctor's chair I mentioned in the introduction?), and He is tweaking your perspective. I hope so. If you are lacking peace and are hungry for His presence in your life in a greater way, maybe you need to practice gratitude. Take a moment to thank Him for 10 things that are good in your life right now. Then get up tomorrow morning and do it again.

AN OBEDIENT HEART

Do you love Jesus? Is it in your heart to follow His ways? I'm guessing the answer is "yes" to both. I am very aware that we are not saved by our works; we are saved by grace through faith, but that doesn't mean it doesn't matter what we do. In John 14 Jesus tells us three ways we can show Him how much we love Him. In verse 15 He says, *"If you love me, you will obey (one) what I command."* And in verse 21 He says it this way, *"Whoever has my commands and obeys (two) them, he is the one who loves me."* And in verse 23 He replied, *"If anyone loves me, he will obey (three) my teaching."*

Ok, don't freak out! None of us are perfect. There is no way we can obey perfectly all of the time. We all sin and fall short of the glory of God, but is it in your heart to obey? Do you have a lifestyle of practicing obedience? When you sense Him convicting you of a bad attitude or rebellious choice, do you repent?

Do you make a change? If so, that's obedience. The goal is to do it the first time, but that isn't always our reality. So maybe it takes us two or three times to get it right ... or sixty or seventy. God is gracious and slow to anger. The point is, do you honor God and His Word above your own wants and desires? David spoke of his love for God's law. He valued it. He also sinned. Big time. It was in his heart to obey, and when he failed, he repented quickly and moved on. He trusted God to forgive him. We won't always get it right. Sometimes we will have to apologize to someone we have hurt, or make a wrong decision right. God doesn't expect perfect. Don't let the enemy condemn you with his evil whispers of doubt and fear when you make a mistake. The Lord is slow to anger, long-suffering and gracious. Repent. Apologize and do what you can to correct a wrong, learn something and move on. Praise Him!

Practically speaking, what does obedience look like? Here are just a few ways that we can honor God daily in response to His great love for us? Are you a reliable, trustworthy friend? Does your "yes" mean "yes"? Do you take the time to help people around you that are in need? Do you go out of your way to express the love of Christ to others in practical ways? I know there have been times in my life when I didn't take the time to see the people around me. I was so busy and focused on what I was doing that I often didn't see the opportunities God put right in front of me. Preferring others ahead of myself is a difficult muscle to strengthen, but I am working on it every time I get into my car or step into line at Costco.

Remember, we are commanded to love the Lord our God above all, but then we are also commanded to love our neighbor as our self. I

"Obedience is an invitation."

recommend we start at home and work our way out. Sometimes it's easy to neglect those closest to us and what a tragedy that can be. If you are involved in serving at church, it can be so easy to let that become your priority. After all, that's what people see. It's harder to do the secret thing—to love, honor and serve when no one else is looking. I hope if anyone in my family reads this they will know that they are my first love, after Jesus.

Obedience is an invitation. Here are a few more habits or disciplines that when developed honor the Lord and invite His presence into your day. I'm going to pitch them at you like baseballs in a batting cage. Ready? Here they come.

Get rid of gossip, even in prayer request form. You know what I'm talking about. Those times when you tell a friend to pray for another friend and then you share the details. Holding on to that juicy information can be torture. That's why if it's none of my business, I don't want to know. Too tempting. I've gossiped too many times. You've probably done it too.

Stop being jealous of that friend who has every-thing and offer a hand to help her with her kids or invite her out for coffee. She doesn't have everything. Trust me.

Stop lying to your husband about how much money you spent today or how many glasses of wine you had. Tell the truth.

Forgive. Forgive. Forgive.

Honor God with your money. Everything we have is a gift from Him. Even the ability to earn money. So, give back to Him first. You get to keep approximately 90% (depending on how you tithe). That's a pretty good deal.

Be quick to listen, slow to speak, and slow to become angry. Ouch! I got a bruise from that one. Perhaps a few hit you between the eyes.

Ephesians 4:19 says, *"Having lost all sensitivity, they have given themselves over to sensuality..."* The things we do and say can and will affect our sensitivity to the Holy Spirit. We can actually give ourselves over to sensuality, or the flesh. If you read further in the chapter, we are warned *"not to grieve the Holy Spirit of God."* Makes sense that if you want more of the Holy Spirit in your life, you should be welcoming to Him, not breaking His heart or bringing Him sorrow. If you want to go deeper, spend some additional time in Ephesians. I recommend taking a few days and reading it several times.

I am not always welcoming to the Holy Spirit. I hate to admit that I'm sure I grieve the Lord often. One thing I struggle with is I have a tendency to be critical of others. Walking into a room, I can make quick judgments about how it's decorated, how those in the room are dressed, if I like the music, food, whatever. I like to think it's a God-given gift, my ability to have an opinion (insert tongue in cheek here). After all, if you needed a "consultant" to come into your church or home, wouldn't you want someone who had a great sense of style and could very quickly give you several ideas to greatly improve it? The problem is, I've never been hired as a consultant and not everybody likes my taste in clothes or decorating or music. You see how this could be a problem? Yes, a pride problem. Thankfully, the older I get, the more I realize how much I don't know. I have learned humility the hard way. By His grace, the Lord is teaching me how to walk this out daily. I have learned that just because I have an opinion, I don't always need to give it, and just because it's mine, doesn't make it right. I'm definitely a work in progress. I still have judgmental thoughts, I just don't usually verbalize them. I trust that God is renewing my mind and gently correcting me when I need it. There is victory in recognizing it, repenting and allowing the Holy Spirit to deal with me regarding my sin.

Walking in humility and embracing humility in your heart is a great way to obey, to express your love for Jesus. You may ask the Lord, "How can I show You that I love You? How can I obey You today?" May I offer these suggestions? Prefer others. Love others. Serve others. As a practical expression, do something for someone today that only they and the Lord will know about, and keep it that way.

> *"All of you, clothe yourselves with humility toward one another, because, "God opposes the proud but gives grace to the humble." Humble yourselves, therefore, under God's mighty hand, that he may lift you up in due time."*
> 1 Peter 5:5-6

If all this talk about obedience has made you uncomfortable and you think I'm starting a Pharisee club, have no fear. Let me say for the record, I hope I have established by now that our motives and the heart behind what we say and do is what's most important. God is so good. He is crazy about us. He desires for us to experience Him every day. Even in times of disobedience, He chases after us. In Psalm 139 it says, *"You see me ... I can never escape from Your Spirit! I can never get away from Your presence"* (NLT). He's good like that. He is always pursuing us and desiring relationship with His kids.

A LOVING HEART

How do I know God is love? When I see the sun streaming through golden and crimson leaves on a brisk fall day, I know God is love. When I hold a baby and see their little toes, perfect in every way, I know God is love. When I hear a song with melodies that makes my heart want to soar, I know God is love. When

I have all of my children around the dinner table, and we are eating and laughing, and my husband and I connect eyes with the understanding that this is what life is all about, I know God is love. When summer is here, and we spend the afternoon relaxing at the beach and enjoying the water, and I open an ice-cold Diet Coke®, I know God is love. (wink)

Seriously, though, I could write for days about the glory and love of God revealed through His creation. The mountains out West, a kiss, the perfect flower, the detail and miracle of a hummingbird or a butterfly. He created it all with you in mind because He loves you with the greatest love of all, demonstrated by sending His Son to earth to become a man, leaving His heavenly fellowship and glory to show us the way to live and ultimately to die for us to make a way.

> *"This is how God showed His love among us: He sent his one and only Son into the world that we might live through Him. This is love; not that we loved God but that He loved us and sent His Son as an atoning sacrifice for our sins. Dear friends, since God so loved us, we also ought to love one another. No one has ever seen God; but if we love one another, God lives in us and His love is made complete in us."*
> *1 John 4:9-12*

In order to maintain a loving heart, we must guard our heart. What exactly is our "heart"? In 1 Samuel 16, when God is rejecting Saul, Samuel says, "The

Lord does not look at the things people look at. People look at the outward appearance, but the Lord looks at the heart." Just as your natural heart is in the center of who you are, so is your spiritual heart the core of who you are. Your heart is what you believe and think, your feelings and desires, the motives behind the choices that you make. The devil wants to steal from you, and the thing he wants most is the understanding of God's love for you deep in your heart. If He can get you to doubt that, he can chip away at your trust in God, and then, he's got you. That's what he did to Eve. He got her to doubt, and a little doubt was all it took. I pray that God will reveal His great love for you today—that you will believe deep down in your heart and soul that God is not holding out on you. If you struggle with being a loving person and it's difficult for you to show love in tangible ways, pray and ask for a love revelation to explode in your life. It seems logical to me that you can only give love to others by the measure you have received love from God. Otherwise, what do you have to give? When we realize that the way we demonstrate love to one another is the predominant way God reveals Himself to the earth, as stated in 1 John, we begin to understand just how important receiving and truly knowing the love of Christ is.

> *"The devil wants to steal from you, and the thing he wants most is the understanding of God's love for you deep in your heart."*

Said another way, having a heart that receives love and gives love is the key to a life filled with the presence of God. He is glorified when we receive His amazing grace, mercy, and love and when we can finally forgive ourselves, realizing that we have already been forgiven. A heart that realizes the miracle of the Father's love can walk in love. A heart forgiven can forgive others and love even their enemies. A life dedicated to loving God and loving people will be a life overflowing with the Spirit. Hopefully, others will see it and want it too.

CAN'T STOP PRAYING

I pray that you will let God reveal Himself to you in a greater measure right now. I agree with Paul as he wrote to the church in Ephesus and said, *"I pray that you, being rooted and established in love, may have power, together will all the saints, to grasp how wide and long and high and deep is the love of Christ, and to know this love that surpasses knowledge-that you may be filled to the measure of all the fullness of God"* Ephesians 3:17-19.

Before we leave the topic of God's love in our hearts, I want to go back to 1 Peter 5:6 where it says to "humble yourselves, under God's mighty hand." Do you find it easy or difficult to picture yourself being under God's hand? The experiences of our childhood can definitely affect our perspectives. When I was young, my mother would "pop us in the mouth" if we talked back or were disrespectful to her. She didn't do it very often because we were such angels, but every once in a while, I would get sassy and quickly receive a little smack on the mouth. I hated it. Getting hit in the face, even though it wasn't very hard, made me draw back every time. Because of this, there were times that she would just reach for the salt or something near me and I would flinch and draw back. She was always surprised by this and puzzled by my overreaction, but I really didn't want to take any chances, so I got out of the way when I could. Fortunately for me, her hands reached for me and held me way more in love then they did in discipline, so I trusted her hand, and in turn, it has made it easier for me to trust God's hand. I realize that my little story of getting hit in the mouth is nothing compared to some of the things people have endured. Perhaps nothing like you have endured. I don't count them as equal, but I use my illustration to make the simple point that sometimes our earthly experiences shape our perspective of or our reaction to God.

I counter that story with an experience I had on a mission trip to India a few years back. I was at a women's conference, and at the end of the message, we had an opportunity to minister to the women. There were so many of them and so few of us, that eventually we stood on the pews and touched as many of them as we could. We would touch the top of their heads and speak a blessing over them or pray a quick prayer. I was so taken back by their response. I found them to be almost like children or puppies, nudging their heads under my hands in request. They wanted the touch and the blessing. It really was a special experience; one I don't take for granted. I can't help compare the two different stories.

What is your response to being under God's mighty hand? Are you hesitant and fearful, waiting to get "popped," or are you eager and pressing in? His love for you is deeper than the sea and higher than the heavens. He wants to heal the wounds that keep you from His love and from His presence. May I encourage you to put on some worship music and sit in His presence? Turn off your phone and breathe, resting in His love. Let Him touch the broken places. Let Him speak to the wounded areas in your heart that keep you guarded and limit His access to your life.

CAN'T GO BACK

I have heard God speak. I am learning to recognize His voice when I hear it (in my mind and spirit). I am learning to trust it. I have felt His presence in times of desperation and pain, and I have experienced Him during times of great joy and laughter. I don't want to live a day without His presence in my life. I can't go back. I can't undo the experience, and now I'm addicted to it.

What's The Point?

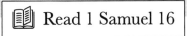 Read 1 Samuel 16

* What is your main takeaway from this chapter?

* David was a man after God's own heart. When we look at his life we see the heart-spirit connection. He knew how to invite and welcome the presence of the Lord. If anyone was addicted to the presence of God, it was David. How about you? Do you desire more of the presence of God in your life?

* What can you practically do in your everyday life to usher in the presence of the Lord?

* Maybe it's something you don't do, or you don't say that makes the Spirit of God more welcome in your day.

* It's an interesting dynamic when it comes to the presence of God. I like to think of it as two sides of the same coin.

* Side 1: God's Spirit lives inside of us. Jesus said it was better for us if He left, so He could send the Comforter to us. (See Romans 8:9-11, John 16:5-16) It is the Spirit of God in us that makes us fruitful. He's the whisper we hear in our inner man, encouraging or instructing us.

* Side 2: The manifest presence of God. When God makes His presence known among us in different ways and in greater levels. (See Exodus 33:14-18, Acts 16:25-26) It is this attribute of His presence I am referring to when I sing, "Come into this place, or show us your glory." His presence is already there because He lives in us. But when He comes into the room in greater measure, you know it.

* Ask God what He wants to say to you today about His presence in your life.

* From my experience, nothing moves the heart of God to come where I am in a greater way, (to manifest His presence) than praise and thanksgiving.

"You are holy, enthroned on the praises of Israel."
Psalm 22:3 (NLV)

SUGGESTED READING

Unveiled by Alan Smith

7

Confession:
I'm Still in Love with My Husband

"Now unto Him who is able to [carry out His purpose and] do superabundantly more than all that we dare ask or think [infinitely beyond our greatest prayers, hopes, or dreams], according to His power that is at work within us."
Ephesians 3:20 (AMP)

Be careful what you ask for. You may get way more than you ever wanted or thought you deserved. I did. I met my husband, Michael, my freshman year of college. He was dating one of my best friends. They dated on and off for several months. At the same time, I liked this other guy. We dated for a while on and off, but he was really in love with this girl from back home, so that was not the best experience. Looking back, I don't know what I was thinking. I should have known liking someone who was in love with someone else would be hard on my heart.

Thankfully, in my sophomore year, I started seeing Michael around campus a lot more. I remember, he was always so genuine and nice to talk to, but he had dated my friend the previous year, so he wasn't really on my radar. At that time, we were what I would call "friendly acquaintances." Then one day in chapel, we were told to pray about three things that were really on our hearts. My first two requests were typical of a college student: provision regarding another mission trip I was scheduled to go on and a good grade for a test I had coming up that week. The third request I remember very well, even to this day, many years later. I was feeling lonely and homesick, and I simply asked the Lord for a companion. Then I left the chapel and went about my day. That night the phone rang, and it was Mike. I was surprised to hear his voice and asked if he wanted to speak to my roommate—as the friend he had dated the previous year was now my roomie. He laughed and said "no," he was calling for me. We went on our first date that night and have been dating ever since. We are getting ready to celebrate our 30th anniversary, and I can honestly say that our life together has been amazing. The Lord, in His infinite wisdom and grace, brought us together that day. Mike will tell you that he was sitting in his room listening to music and told his roommate out of the blue, "I think I'm going to call Teri." He said it wasn't really something he planned to do; it was like he was compelled to do it. But I know why. (Wink)

Our life together has been a gift from God; that's for sure. We've had, and continue to have, a wonderful romance filled with times of great joy and love, but we have also endured seasons of pain and struggle, busyness and regret. Seasons change, sometimes so quickly and with such force, it can take you by surprise. We've done life together these past thirty years and endured many kinds of weather. You never really know what tomorrow holds, do you? One day it's sunny and warm and the next it's stormy and dark, and it feels like the rain is never going to end. I can honestly say that each trial of life has brought us closer to one another, developed our maturity and depth, and given us a greater understanding of who God is. Most people are looking for someone to love them; we were both looking for someone to love. I think that difference has been the secret to our relationship and what has brought us through every season of life. So far.

> *"Seasons change, sometimes so quickly and with such force, it can take you by surprise."*

SPRING (THE FIRST 10 YEARS)

We married young; I was still in school, and Mike was a graduate assistant. Those early years were so much fun. We were broke, but we didn't care. We ate hot dogs for dinner a lot (mostly because I didn't know how to cook). After my graduation, we moved to Michigan so I could be near my family when we started ours. I got a job in advertising, and Mike began his career in pharmaceutical sales. We had several years together of enjoying our work and each other. We were spontaneous; we traveled, and we really got to know each other well during those years. It wasn't until we had a minor health scare 2 ½ years in that we discovered we had a much greater health issue to deal with than we originally thought.

In a nutshell, we were staring straight into the hollow, dark eyes of infertility. This was a shock for both of us, to say the least. We had stayed pure before marriage, but that didn't seem to matter in this area of life. This was not a matter of reaping fruit, good or bad. It just was the situation. Sometimes life just happens. The doctors didn't give us much hope because with our situation there wasn't much they could do medically. We began to pray. We went to specialists and continued to pray. After a year or so, we found ourselves sitting across the desk from the best infertility doctor at the Cleveland Clinic. We were so hopeful, waiting for him to tell us that he had the one answer that no one else had. He didn't. He said, "Well, I hope you believe in miracles because that's what it's going to take. There is nothing we can do for you." I remember sitting there stunned. Looking back, I am grateful that he was so blunt. His words, as hard as they were to hear, made me stop and think.

I replied after a few seconds, "Well, we do. So thank you for your time."

Did we really believe in miracles? It's one thing to say you do and a totally different thing to live like it when the word "impossible" is staring you in the face. As the years went by, the emptiness inside me grew. Mike and I were happy together, but neither of us pictured our lives without children. After several years of praying and believing, I remember being so tired of praying about our situation that when I felt like I wanted to take it to the Lord again, I would just throw up a "You know" and leave it at that. Other times I would get frustrated and forcefully remind God that His Word told me to be fruitful and multiply. I would also remind Him of the miracle we needed in order to obey what He said to do. I can remember reading the story of Hannah in 1 Samuel … a lot. It always brought me comfort, as I was reminded each time that not only did God hear Hannah's cry for a child, but He answered her and gave her a child that was destined to do great things for His kingdom. Reminding myself of what God did for Hannah brought hope to my spirit, as I know that God is no respecter of persons. If He did it for her, He could do it for me.

During this season of infertility, frustration, and faith, peace and sadness would take turns rolling over me like waves. I couldn't really control what wave was going to hit me; I could only respond to it. After years of treading water out among the waves of emotion, I finally learned that surrender was the only thing that would keep my head above water. Fighting and stressing only made me choke and begin to sink. Fortunately, during those years, we had many people praying for us. My mother and sister came along side us and stood faithfully in the gap with prayer and support. My sister, Cherie, never doubted that the Lord would give us children. She had total faith and peace about it. I was grateful that the Lord had given this amazing assurance to her, but I wished He would have given a little to me too. I'm grateful that our family and friends prayed and believed even when we couldn't.

During those years of waiting, praying, and trusting, it got difficult to go to church. I was so conflicted because, as you know by now, I love to go to church, but going only accentuated my barrenness. If you've never struggled with infertility or ever known someone who has, you probably don't realize that it is at church where family is best on display. The laughter, the cute little outfits, the mom's holding their babies while worshiping. That was hard to be around. And forget about church on Mother's Day. That's when I would throw up another "You know" and keep moving.

One day in August of 1991, my sister was praying again for us on her way to work—as she was in the habit of doing—when the Holy Spirit stopped her and told her it was done. She could stop asking. That same weekend while mother was folding towels, she too was praying for us and felt the Lord tell her in her spirit that I would have multiple births. It was done. The two of them called each other in excitement but waited to see. Meanwhile, that weekend Mike and I went to Cedar Point, an amusement park in Ohio that we loved visiting. While on the first ride, I almost passed out. That had never happened to me. I felt a little funny the whole day but didn't know why. When we came back from our vacation, I thought that maybe it might be true. But did I dare take a test and get a negative result – again? I mustered up the courage and took a pregnancy test. Sure enough, it was positive. I immediately went to the doctor to take a blood test to confirm the results. God had worked a miracle, and after three years of trying, we were going to have a miracle baby! I must confess, I did a little dance in the waiting room when they gave me the results.

Funny thing, when I invited my mom and sister over to give them the big news, they didn't seem as surprised and excited as I thought they would be. That's because they already knew— those little stinkers. They were as excited to share their news with me as I was to share mine with them. Looking back through the years, I've often wondered why we had to go through that trial. God could have healed us before we even knew there was a problem, or He could have immediately answered when we called upon His name. What was the point of it all? There have been times when I thought that

> *"I'm always so amazed at how God can benefit so many people and situations with one move of His hand."*

maybe the Lord needed to soften us to be the parents our children would need us to be. I know that we were and are different parents than we would have been without the infertility struggle, that's for sure. We may never truly know what He worked in us and out of us during those years, but I think it is more than that. Sometimes it's just not about us. Sometimes God uses us and our situations to affect other situations and other people. Looking back, I think our infertility was as much for my sister as it was for me. She encountered the Lord and her faith grew. Nothing and no one can ever take the experience of hearing God's voice away from Cherie. It marked her. What I love so much about the way God works is that it doesn't matter whether or not it was Cherie's journey or Him working in us that was His primary focus. God never wastes anything. Just because He's working in you and your circumstance doesn't mean He can't use your situation to minister to or affect others, and vice versa. I'm always so amazed at how God can benefit so many people and situations with one move of His hand.

After giving birth to Carli, our miracle baby, 15 months later we were gifted with another unexpected miracle when Mallory was born. And three years after that, I delivered our third miracle baby, who we named Nicholas. Amazing that we had to put a stop to all of the miracles. What a nice surprise.

Mallory reminded me recently of a message she heard while away at college that really ministered to her during a dry, empty time in her own life. The message's focus was on the idea that from barrenness comes greatness. Sarah, Elizabeth, and Hannah are just a few examples of women who could not conceive, but out of their longing came some of the most memorable and influential people in the Bible. God used the truth from that message to touch a tender place in Mallory's heart with the realization that she too was conceived from barrenness and that He has great things in store for her as well. God never wastes anything. Ever.

SUMMER (THE SECOND 10 YEARS)

Be careful what you wish for. You may get it. When I had Nicholas, Carli was four, and Mallory had just turned three. I believe that I only sat down five times that whole year. Of course, I'm exaggerating, but it sure did feel that way. I was a stay-at-home mom, and I really did love it. I realize that staying home is not for everyone, but we agreed that whatever Mike made was what we would live on. I did consider going back to work about a year after having Nic. My former employer wanted to hire me on a contract basis to do some employee training (something I enjoyed doing very much). It was ideal, but it just wasn't for me. The few times I went in, I just wanted to be at the playland with my kids. For well over 10 years, I didn't work outside the home because raising my kids kept me very busy.

Busyness is the word I would use to describe the summer years. Band concerts, Pee Wee football through high school Varsity, T-ball that turned into softball, dance class, puppet ministry, basketball, piano lessons, etc. Sound familiar? We tried to expose our kids to all kinds of activities hoping that they would find their specific interests and gifting. Among all of these activities, we were also involved at church on Sunday and Wednesday nights. I use the term we loosely, though. During these years, Mike was very busy with work. He traveled a lot, and even when he was home, he was working out of his home office. Don't get me wrong; Mike has always been engaged at home. Back then, he was just very busy and away from home a lot. Looking back, we were all busy and away from home a lot.

As the kids got busier and life got more hectic, I was faced with a choice: how was I going to handle being a part-time "single" mom? Now, to all of you single moms, please hang in there with me. I know that my experience cannot compare to yours. I have such amazing respect and compassion for the single moms I know. They are true champions of selflessness. But when you are married, you don't expect to be home alone and parenting on your own for extended periods of time. Ah, so now I have exposed the root of the issue. I was dealing with unmet expectations. At first, when Mike began to get busier with work and travel a great deal, I did ok, but after a little while, the novelty wore off, and I dealt with feelings of resentment and frustration. In those moments when my shirt had spit-up on it, and my hair was in a ponytail for the third day in a row, and I was exhausted, I was presented with a choice. Either I believed in the call of God on Mike's life, or I didn't. And I either believed that God had provided us with his job and that Mike was doing the best he could for our family and his career, or I wasn't. I realized that I did believe Mike was doing his best, and I admired his amazing work ethic. The very thing that originally attracted me to him was now frustrating me. It's interesting how that works sometimes. I still admire his amazing work ethic. I don't know anyone who is more honest and hardworking than my husband.

During those very busy years and inspired by the situation in which I found myself, I had my first idea for a book. I was going to call it *When Kings Go off to War - A Woman's Guide to Thriving When Her Husband Travels*. I imagined the cover had a picture of a man in a suit holding a briefcase standing by a mirror near his front door getting ready to leave. His reflection was that of a warrior, maybe like a medieval knight or a Braveheart kind of character. Just as the men of King David's day went off to war, being away from home has become part of the job description for many men of our generation as well. Some things never change. As I mentioned, I was presented with a choice. I could resent and resist, or I could accept and pray. After doing a bit of both, I made up my mind to be on "Team Mike." This shift in my thinking changed my expectations and brought peace to my heart and to our family. Perhaps you find yourself in a similar situation or know someone who is, or maybe you're equally busy working to take care of the family. Either way, some of these truths could apply to your situation.

Here are a few tips from my notes from *When Kings Go off to War*.

- **Get on board:** Do you know what your husband does for a living? I mean, really know? Do you know what he enjoys about it, or what keeps him up at night? If not, that's a great place to start. It's natural to have a "me vs. him" mentality if you don't understand the reason for his having to leave—again. When my husband explained what he was doing and what was expected of him by his employer, it helped me to be more empathetic to his situation. If your husband is gone more than you would like, has that been communicated to him? And I'm not talking about you yelling and complaining about it; that just breeds guilt and stress in him. Perhaps, if you talked about it, you would discover that the situation may be temporary or has the potential for change if you share with him how his leaving so often affects you. Maybe you will discover that this temporary travel or overtime can lead to a promotion and that could bring agreement between you that the sacrifice is worth the potential reward. Whatever you discover, the bottom line is that you must communicate with one another, and when each person in the marriage knows that the other person is not only for them but also is giving them the benefit of the doubt, it really helps. Communication starts with you because your husband isn't reading this book; you are. I feel I need to add one last thought, though. Maybe your husband isn't interested in communicating with you. Perhaps you've had conversations that haven't gone well, and you've learned to leave well enough alone. If that's you, don't give up friend. Pray. Respond to life the best you can and continue to pray for him and the situation. Tell God all about it and ask Him for what you want, because sometimes "you have not because you ask not." As for me, during those tired, busy, early days, I had to learn to be content in my situation, but it was a process.

- **Girl power:** Get yourself some girlfriends. Your husband can't meet all of your needs. A strong support system is essential, especially if your kids are young and depend on you for everything. Years ago, when I knew a trip was coming up and Mike would be gone for four or five days, I would make a plan. On day two or three, I would either have a friend over with her kids, or I would go shopping with my mom, or I would schedule a sitter and a friend and I would go to dinner or a movie. It didn't really matter what we did, being with another adult and having adult conversations helped to break up the monotony. I anticipated the emotions that might come during his time away and met them head on before they could get a hold of me. (Resist the opportunity to let these times become husband-bashing sessions. Protect and honor your husband, just as you would want him to protect and honor you.)

- **Get plugged in:** John 15 talks about abiding in the vine. As stated before, your husband cannot be your source. Jesus must be your source. Remaining in the True Vine, Jesus, is the only way to live a fruitful life. How can you give life and love to others unless you are daily going to the source? We give, we leak, and we get empty real fast. Don't put pressure on those around you to always be filling up your tank. Let the Giver of Life, be the one you go to daily. We don't pray and read, study and grow because God demands it; we do it because it benefits us and those around us. I don't know about you, but I want to be a fruitful tree, strong and healthy, so my family can come to me and be refreshed.

- **Keep it interesting:** Do you do things to promote growth in your own life? Do you have interests outside your home that excite and motivate you? It doesn't matter what it is. People are attracted to people that are excited about life and motivated to do something. Your husband is a person too. I know that is an obvious statement to make, but I think sometimes we don't expect our husbands to respond like people. We hold them to a higher standard and expect them to be attracted to us no matter what we do, or don't do. That's not fair. Ladies, give your man a reason to want to come home and a reason to be sad when he has to leave. That's all I'm saying about that.

FALL (THE PAST 10 YEARS)

What a joy the past 10 years have been. Football games, family vacations, kids getting their drivers licenses, graduations and so much more. I remember saying when my kids were young, "I just want to be able to go out to dinner and have my kids be able to cut their own meat and wipe their own butts." Well, I did get my wish eventually. All of our children have grown to become talented, kind, adventurous, loving people. There has been much joy and sometimes heartache in watching our children struggle to discover who they are going to be. I am thrilled with the young adults they have become, but the process of letting them go took me by surprise.

We are becoming empty-nesters. Carli has been out on her own for some time now, and even though Mallory is a college graduate, she is home visiting for a while until she gets on her feet. Although Nic is away at college now, he still comes home on the weekends once in a while, dirty laundry in tow. Slowly letting them go has been a challenge for me and allowing my children to reap the consequences of their decisions is the hardest thing I've ever had to do. I think if I would have practiced this more when they were young it would have made it easier for me to watch when the consequences became more significant. Looking back, I realize that I often buffered my kids to minimize the pain they would experience. By doing this, I didn't do them any favors. I didn't do myself any either.

Currently, I'm trying to prepare myself for the day when there are no kids around as the Christmas tree goes up. Mallory and I enjoyed the process together this year, but I was very aware that it may just be me and hubby next year. Season's change and we will take them as they come. This Christmas will be the first time we won't all be together. Carli is back at Hillsong Church in Sydney. I'm so proud of her for daring to live on the other side of the world. She is learning so much and growing into such an amazing young woman, but she will be wearing sunglasses and a tee shirt on the beach with friends this year, not drinking hot chocolate with us as we enjoy the snow. Season's change. I choose to embrace that fact when the lonely pangs hit my stomach. I know that God's got me— that He sees me.

My sweet momma is one step ahead of me. I see her living on her own without my father, who we lost to Parkinson's disease a few years ago. She too struggles with feelings of loneliness, as is expected after such a great loss. When she and I get together, sometimes we talk about the feelings of loss, as hard as it is, and in those times we cling to each other and Jesus. When everything is stripped away and everyone goes home, isn't that who we've held on to all along?

So what am I doing to combat the emptiness that accompanies this season of my life? I'm writing a book. I'm thinking of you and the potential of us journeying together. I'm pressing into God and continuing to learn and grow. I'm reaching out, helping those in need with less time on their hands. I'm praying that God will lead me to the next step and shine the light of His love on my face.

As I end this chapter, I must confess that I'm still very much in love with my husband. Our marriage hasn't been perfect, but who wants perfect anyway? I'll take the laughter that comes from imperfection any day. Our life together has been a gift. One for which I am very grateful. We've spent many hours on our knees together praying for God to intervene on our behalf. We've taken our children to church with joy and expectation. We've traveled and made memories—laughed a lot and cried some too. It's been good. God knew what I needed more than I did. He saw two people ready to love and be loved and drew us together. I'm really looking forward to the next 30 years.

What's The Point?

📖 Read Ecclesiastes 3

* What is your main takeaway from this chapter?

* *"He has made everything beautiful in its time"*
  Ecclesiastes 3:11. That's God's way of saying hind-
  sight is 20/20. When we look back on a season in
  our life, we gain perspective. Somehow the dis-
  tance from that time and place helps us to see the
  experience with fresh eyes. But man, when you're
  in the middle of it, when you're going through
  the cancer treatments, or sending that resume
  again, or waiting for the right person to come
  along, it can be hard to find the good. This truth
  about perspective is also true of the good times.
  We tend to take people and places for granted,
  and it's not until our situation has changed, that
  we truly see what a precious gift those moments
  and those people were.

* How would you describe the season you are currently in?

* What would you change about your current circumstances if you could?

* Imagine for a moment that you are looking back on your life as it is right now. What could be the sweet surprise that you might not be currently seeing?

* Once again I am reminded of my parents, when my dad seemed to age all of a sudden way quicker than my mom. Those days were difficult for both of them; however, I know she would treasure sitting with him at the assisted living facility, drinking a bad cup of coffee, while watching the Tigers beat the Red Sox one more time.

* Do you know someone who is currently going through a difficult season? What can you do to reach out to them?

* Ask the Holy Spirit to give you someone to love on today. May I encourage you to make yourself available to God? You'll be amazed at how quickly He puts you in the path of a hurting person. He loves to love on His children. He uses us to do it. Are you willing to be used today?

"I will exalt you, O Lord; for you lifted me out of the depths and did not let my enemies gloat over me. O Lord my God, I called to you for help and you healed me. O Lord, you brought me up from the grave; you spared me from going down into the pit. Sing to the Lord, you saints of his; praise his holy name. For his anger lass only a moment, but His favor lasts a lifetime; weeping may remain for a night, but rejoicing comes in the morning."
Psalm 30:1-5

SUGGESTED READING

———

Think Differently Live Differently
by Bob Hamp

8

Confession:
I Don't Think About the Devil Much

"Be self-controlled and alert. Your enemy the devil prowls around like a roaring lion looking for someone to devour."
1 Peter 5:8

I've recently realized that I like to live in denial. I find it comforting. If I can deny the reality of something, it can't hurt me. It makes sense why when I see myself in a photo lately, I'm a little surprised because surely that's not what I really look like. I haven't really gained 10 pounds, right? Ok, maybe 20. It also explains the credit card debt that has recently snuck up on me. How did that happen? Denial. A few years ago, my best friend announced she was moving to South Carolina, and I wasn't as upset as my other friends. I think at the time I credited myself with being well adjusted and spiritual. I wasn't either; I was living in denial. Deep down, I think I figured she and her family wouldn't really move. I assumed that something would happen to keep them here. Once they actually moved, I believed it wouldn't be for long, or at least that's what I told myself. They moved over two years ago, and I'm just making peace with the fact that she's gone. I like to tell myself she will be back. They will miss us here too much to stay there. A job will bring them "home." Denial. So, let me state for the record, my friend Emily lives in South Carolina, and as far as I know, she and her family are not coming back to Michigan anytime soon. Ok … now I can cry. Better late than never.

REALITY

Knowing my propensity for denial might explain why I have never spent much time thinking about the devil. Why would I want to contemplate the reality that I have an enemy who wants to devour me? I would much rather spend my time and energy focusing on a Savior that loves me and has a plan for my life. While that is an important fact to focus on, it is foolish to ignore or deny that God has an enemy that hates me and not only hates me, but would love to kill me because when he looks at me, he sees Jesus living in me. I can no longer deny the fact that I am in a war. The reality is, I am in a war every day, and if I'm smart, I will "put on" the armor given to me to live victoriously.

Any thought that is contrary to the Word of God is from the enemy, always.

For a moment, let's look at what the Bible tells us about the devil. In John 8:44, Jesus himself tells us that Satan is a *"murderer from the beginning, not holding to the truth, for there is no truth in him. When he lies, he speaks his native language, for he is a liar and the father of lies."* Well, that's quite a description. Paul tells us that he is a schemer in 2 Corinthians 2:10, *"If there was anything to forgive -I have forgiven in the sight of Christ for your sake, in order that Satan might not outwit us. For we are not unaware of his schemes."* Make a mental note of the context, as we will come back to it. Forgiving others is what Paul is talking about here. The devil would love for us to be unforgiving and hold bitterness in our hearts. I think it brings him joy (if he can experience joy). In Zechariah 3 and Revelation 12, he is described as our accuser. He actually stands before the throne of God accusing us. He's got some nerve. Did you know that the name Satan means accuser? If we go all of the way back to Genesis 3, we see he is described as the serpent, and the first lie he convinced Eve of, he is still using on us today. And he continues to be successful. I guess he knows, if it's not broke, don't fix it. Remember the conversation in Genesis 3:1-4? *"Did God really say, 'You must not eat from any tree in the garden? The woman said to the serpent, "We may eat fruit from the trees in the garden," but God did say, 'You must not eat fruit from the tree that is in the middle of the garden, and you must not touch it, or you will die?'" "You will not surely die," the serpent said to the* woman. *"For God knows that when you eat of it your eyes will be opened, and you will be like God, knowing good and evil."* Simply put, he convinced her that God was not to be trusted and was holding out on her. He still uses that with us today, and we believe him too. I could go on and on with scriptures about who our enemy is, but honestly, I don't want to dedicate any more time to him. I will say this, and I believe scripture supports it, all brutality, sickness, fear, anxiety, darkness, depression, murder, envy, lust, etc., are all from him. Any thought that is contrary to the Word of God is from the enemy—always.

So, we agree there is a devil and that he is our enemy. And perhaps now we are reminded of who and what we are dealing with a little bit better. Living in denial or burying our head in the sand as it pertains to Satan is foolish. Hosea 4:6 says, *"My people are destroyed from lack of knowledge."* And down in 4:14 it says, *"A people without understanding will come to ruin."* Ok, ok, I get it. I need to know what the Word says about this battle we are in. Great news, though! We are not left to ourselves to fight this mighty foe. We know from 1 John 4:4, *"The one who is in you is greater than the one who is in the world."* So, because of Jesus Christ, he isn't a mighty foe at all. He no longer holds power over us. We have the Holy Spirit living inside of us, and we have authority by the blood and name of Jesus to resist him. We do need to resist him though. I'm learning that I can't ignore him any longer.

THINK ABOUT IT

I think because some people have given too much credit to the devil, I don't like to give him any. Have you ever known someone who is always talking about being under attack? It's like they want to give him credit for everything. That drives me crazy. I like what my pastor says, "Sometimes it's not Satan; it's just stupid." Now that's funny (and true). We are continually reaping what we have sown, good or bad. The decisions we make today, big and small, will affect our lives in the future. Financial decisions, physical decisions, relationship decisions, etc. Sometimes when we find ourselves in the hospital, it's a result of a destructive behavior we have nurtured for years. Now the devil most likely whispered that temptation in our ear over and over again to encourage that behavior. I will admit to giving him credit for that, but ultimately, many times it's our choices that take us down a destructive or productive path.

Joyce Meyer says the battlefield is in the mind. I know this is true. 2 Corinthians 10:5 says, *"We demolish arguments and every pretension that sets itself up against the knowledge of God, and we take captive every thought to make it obedient to Christ."* I don't know about you, but I am still working on that skill. Making my mind obey, training it to think on purpose and not just be open to every thought that makes its way in there is difficult. Bob Hamp, author of *Think Differently Live Differently*, has an illustration for this that I just love. He says something like this, "We are vulnerable to the songs we know from our past. I never wake up with a rap song playing in my head." Me either Bob. "I don't listen to rap, so it's never in my head; however, if I hear a song on the radio that I like or was from my childhood, I may find myself singing it later in the day, remembering every word because it's one that I know." Bob says that is what the devil does. He picks a "song" from our past and just starts humming the first line. We take it from there. For instance, "You're ugly. You'll never amount to anything." "You're dumb, why are you even trying?" "Don't get your hopes up; remember what happened last time?" Perhaps someone you loved or respected spoke to you like that. A parent, a teacher, or a classmate. You hear it again in your mind and believe it. Believing the lie makes it really easy for the devil to get that message/song playing in your head, again. He just gets the song started, and you take it from there. I have done that, for sure, but I'm learning to recognize the difference between the devil and his lies and the truth of God. Most times, when I have negative thoughts plaguing my mind, I take credit for those thoughts. I am learning to give credit to the father of lies, my accuser. I am learning to change the dial of my mind to another station, one that is playing songs of truth. I am also learning that I get to choose. I am not a victim to my thought life. I like what the Bible says about this in Colossians 3:1-3, *"Therefore if you have been raised with Christ [to a new life, sharing in His resurrection from the dead], keep seeking the things that are above, where Christ is, seated at the right hand of God. Set your mind and keep focused habitually on the things above [the heavenly things], not on things that are on the earth [which have only temporal value]. For you died [to this world], and your [new, real] life is hidden with Christ in God"* (AMP).

We must begin to take thoughts captive and replace them with truth. It's not easy. Most times I am unaware that I am even thinking a destructive thought. I just know I am feeling sad or lonely or scared. If you can relate, let your feelings be the clue you need to change your thoughts. After a time of practicing this technique of matching feelings with thoughts, you will begin to recognize a lie of the enemy and change your thoughts before the feelings ever come. I would like to use Romans 12:1-2 as a prayer guide for us today.

"Father God, we offer our bodies as living sacrifices, holy and pleasing to you in worship. Help us, Father, to no longer conform to the ways of this world, to think like this world, but to be changed and transformed to be like You by the renewing of our minds so that we can know Your voice and know what Your will is for our lives. We trust that Your will for us is good and perfect. In Jesus' name, Amen."

SHINE THE LIGHT

In his book *Victory Over the Darkness*, Neil Anderson says, "Because Satan's primary weapon is the lie, your defense against him is the truth. Dealing with Satan is not a power encounter; it is a truth encounter. When you expose Satan's lie with God's truth, his power is broken."[7] That is why Jesus said, "You shall know the truth and the truth shall set you free." In John 14:6

Jesus tells us, *"I am the way and the truth and the life. No one comes to the Father except through me."* Truth is a person—Jesus. Neil goes on to say, "Satan's lie cannot withstand the truth any more than the darkness of night can withstand the light of the rising sun. We are not called to dispel the darkness; we are called to turn on the light." Did you catch

> *"Dealing with Satan is not a power encounter; it is a truth encounter."*

that? We are called to turn on—or be—the light. If we live this reality, won't it change the way we live? "To bring the light" is something I can do. Dispelling the darkness is overwhelming because I wasn't called to do it. The light will take care of the darkness. I love this truth. I think of social media when I read this. How many people try to "fix" or correct the darkness? Instead, all we are required to do is bring the light, to be the light.

If you get nervous thinking about spiritual warfare, I understand. It's real. More real than I ever wanted to admit. But never fear. Fear is from the enemy. If he can keep you afraid, he's got you. It's kind of funny that "fear not" is in the Bible 365 times. One for every day of the year. If we know the truth (remember that Jesus is the Truth) and if we know who we are in Him, we never have to be afraid. We need only to shine the light of Christ on our situation and the atmosphere around us, and the devil has to flee.

Paul had to deal with a "messenger of Satan, to torment him." You can read about it in 2 Corinthians 12:8, and even Jesus had to deal with the devil. Before He began His ministry, He was led by the Holy Spirit into the desert where He fasted and prayed for 40 days and was then tempted by the devil. It was God's will for Him to deal with the enemy. Could it be God's will for us to be tested and tried by the devil as well? As strange as that thought may be, I believe it is. I don't pretend to fully understand why God allows the devil to exist. If I ran the world, I would cast him into outer darkness now and get it over with. But I do know this: love must offer a choice, and if everything was perfect and always worked out perfectly for us, would we need to choose to believe? The fact that my husband continues to love me when no one is forcing him too, not even society, makes it all the more wonderful that he still does. He gets to make the choice every day if he is going to stay engaged and committed or if he is going to begin to look the other way. I love the scene in the movie Bruce Almighty when God tells Bruce that He can't make anyone love him. It must be a choice of their free will. Then, later in the movie, Bruce goes on to understand that same reality with his girlfriend Grace, and it is his sacrificial love for her that moves God. I know it's just a movie, but it demonstrates the point so well.

If Jesus and Paul had to deal with the devil, why wouldn't we have to deal with him too? However, we see in the book of Job that Satan had to go through

God to get to Job, so it stands to reason that he has to go through God to get to you and me too. This brings me comfort because I trust God. Satan? Not so much. Thankfully, Jesus gives us an example of how to deal with the devil. It's important that we recognize that it really isn't much of a battle. Jesus knew who He was and the authority He had. He spoke The Word in response to the devil's temptations, for He is the Word. He responded to the devil from a place of truth. Remember what Neil said, "Dealing with Satan is not a power encounter; it's a truth encounter." We have the authority because we have the truth.

Something else to consider: we see many examples in the Bible where the enemy brings things into our lives to harm us and then God uses them for our good. The story of Joseph being thrown into a pit by his brothers and left to die, only to make his way to the palace in Egypt, illustrates this point beautifully. I have found this to be true in my life as well. Times of great trial and desperation have ushered in great encounters with the Lord. They have taken me to places I would have never normally gone and have revealed His ways to me in greater depth.

So, what is the truth about me? What is the truth about you? If we are to be able to put the devil in his place when he charges at our families and us with his threats and accusations, we need to know not only who we are but also whose we are.

WHO WE ARE: WE ARE CARRIERS OF HIS PRESENCE AND HIS POWER

- *Colossians 1:27 speaks of "Christ in you, the hope of glory."*

- *1 John 4:4 says, "the One who is in you is greater than the one who is in the world."*

- *Ephesians 1:18-19 (condensed): "I pray also that the eyes of your heart may be enlightened in order that you may know...His incomparably great power for us who believe. That power is like the working of His mighty strength which he exerted in Christ when he raised him from the dead and seated him at his right hand in the heavenly realms, far above all rule and authority, pwer and dominion."*

- *Romans 6:11: "and hope does not disappoint us, because God has poured out his love into our hearts by the Holy Spirit, whom he has given us."*

- *1 Corinthians 6:19: "Do you not know that your body is the temple of the Holy Spirit, who is in you, whom you have received from God?"*

- *Colossians 2:9-10: "For in Christ all the fullness of the Deity lives in bodily form, and you have been given fullness in Christ, who is the head over every power and authority."*

- *2 Timothy 1:7: "God did not give us a spirit of timidity/ fear, but a spirit of power, of love and of self-discipline/ sound mind."*

WHOSE WE ARE: WE HAVE BEEN GIVEN AUTHORITY AS CHILDREN OF GOD

- *Matthew 28:18: "All authority in heaven and on earth has been given to me. Therefore go…"*

- *Luke 10:19: "I have given you authority to trample on snakes and scorpions and to overcome all the power of the enemy; nothing will harm you."*

- *Romans 8:15-17: "For you did not receive a spirit that makes you a slave to fear but you received the Spirit of sonship. And by Him we cry, 'Abba Father.' The Spirit himself testifies with our spirit that we are God's children. Now if we are God's children, then we are heirs- heirs of God and co-heirs with Christ…"*

- *1 Peter 2:9: "You are a chosen people, a royal priesthood, a holy nation, a people belonging to God, that you may declare the praises of him who called you out of darkness into his wonderful light."*

- *James 5:16: "The prayer of a righteous man/woman is powerful and effective."*

- *Ephesians 2:6: "And God raised us up with Christ and seated us with Him in the heavenly realms in Christ Jesus."*

RESIST, AND KEEP RESISTING

These truths are amazing! How amazing is the position we hold as followers of Christ? We are family, heirs together with Jesus. God raised us and seated us with Him in the heavens. It's done. We are seated with Him now in the Spirit. This reality must affect our view of spiritual warfare. We must know who we are and whose we are if we are to speak to the enemy and his demons with truth, power and authority.

We are in a battle with an enemy that is real and out to steal our health, our peace, our effectiveness, and our joy, but we have been given the truth to resist him and live a victorious life. Sometimes the battle is overcome quickly, but other times it's a process. What do we do then? I recently heard Louie Giglio giving his testimony on James and Betty Robison's television show Life Today. I have to admit; I was a little surprised. He was sharing about his battle with depression and how for a couple of months he thought he was losing his mind—this from one of America's most influential and anointed voices. Louie is the founder of the Passion movement. Thousands of young people have come and continue to come to know the Lord through his ministry. In the interview, he spoke of how overwhelmed he became during a very busy and emotional season in his life. One night he woke up and thought he was dying. An overwhelming fear and dread came over him, and for months he was incapacitated. He prayed, he had others pray, he claimed scripture and still in the darkness of night he experienced what he described as a cloud that would fill his heart and mind with anxiety and dread. His experience was lengthy and greatly affected his health and life. When telling his story, he quoted Jesus in

John 16 when He tells the disciples, *"I have told you these things, so that in me you may have peace. In this world you will have trouble. But take heart! I have overcome the world."* He had trouble all right. It reminds me of something else my pastor says, "This isn't heaven." His momma told him that. We will all encounter difficult storms—it's only a matter of time. (Yippee!) What ultimately brought Louie through that storm was prayer and worship. One night, when he was at his lowest point, he called out to God again and cried out for help. He was reminded of the scripture in Isaiah 61:3 where it says to exchange a *"garment of praise instead of a spirit of despair."* So he asked God for a song and God gave him one. He began to sing that song of God's healing, loving arms and eventually the oppression slowly left. Louie said that "worship lights up the tunnel." Darkness can't exist in the light, remember? The devil and his demons can't stand the sound. Louie said that he realized that he is prone to that spirit of fear/anxiety, so he is careful to recognize the lie when it comes and to keep his focus on the right thing—Jesus.

You may have a similar story. I do. Years ago, Mike and I went through a season where we began to experience a presence, and it wasn't God's. It only came at night and it brought anxiety and fear with it. We did what we knew to do: we prayed, declared scripture, sang a new song (and a few old songs) to the Lord. Some nights we resisted and were able to go right back to sleep, and other nights one or both of us would get up and pray and read our Bible to refocus our thoughts on the truth. This happened for several months, and then finally we realized that we weren't waking up as often anymore. Eventually, we weren't waking up at all. I'm not sure what opened the door to that spirit, and I'm not sure what specific thing finally brought the victory, but I know that when we sensed the presence of the enemy, we resisted and he eventually left, but it was a battle. Somehow it brought me comfort to know that Louie, such a wonderful man of God, faced a similar trial. That's why I'm writing this book. We've got to be real. We've got to tell our stories. We all need to know that we are not alone. We need to declare the faithfulness and goodness of God. Thank you, Louie, for sharing your story. I'm so glad you are better and back to helping others.

STAND YOUR GROUND

The battle is real. Thankfully, we know that God did not leave us defenseless. I can't live in denial any longer. It's time to engage in the fight. Paul's letter to the Ephesians is my favorite letter, and he equips his listeners masterfully. It's full of great prayers, encouragement and wisdom. The letter to the Ephesians ends with Paul admonishing the people. He says, *"Be strong in **the Lord** and in **His mighty power**"* Ephesians 6:10 (emphasis mine to highlight that we do not have to do the work, He does). While I'm realizing that I play a greater part in the fight than I previously thought, and I want to inspire us to engage and be prepared, I want you to know that I write about our part in the battle with caution. As I've said in previous chapters, I don't want to give us a list of things to do to try harder. What we need is a revelation. I know too many controlling, fretting, striving people looking for another list of things to "do." So, as you read this next section, know that I am writing to the ladies that like to have a to-do list—the achievers who struggle with letting go and letting God, myself included.

First, let's take another look at Ephesians 6:11-17:

> *"Put on the full armor of God, so that you can take your stand against the devil's schemes. For our struggle is not against flesh and blood, but against the rulers, against the authorities, against the powers of this dark world and against the spiritual forces of evil in the heavenly realms. Therefore put on the full armor of God, so that when the day of evil comes, you may be able to stand your ground, and after you have done everything, to stand. Stand firm then, with the belt of truth buckled around your waist, with the breastplate of righteousness in place, and with your feet fitted with the readiness that comes from the gospel of peace. In addition to all this, take up the shield of faith, with which you can extinguish all the flaming arrows of the evil one. Take the helmet of salvation and the sword of the Spirit, which is the word of God."*

How do we take our stand against the devil's schemes? We cover ourselves with armor. That is our responsibility; the heavy lifting is up to the Lord. The battle is the Lord's. I know we are told to "put on" the armor, but isn't it already on us and inside of us? It's the Pez vs. piñata concept. Perhaps when you read to put on the helmet of salvation, you feel as if it's something you need to get from a closet or pull down off a shelf, but you don't. It's already on your head if Jesus is your Lord and Savior. May I suggest for our discussion here, that we use the term access instead of put on. Sometimes when I think of myself putting on the armor of God, I feel more like a young David putting on Saul's armor, rather than Wonder Woman strong and fearless. If putting on the armor seems cumbersome to you, maybe unrealistic for everyday life, remember … Jesus lives in you. Jesus is (the belt of) Truth and He is our (breastplate of) Righteousness. He is the (gospel of peace) Prince of Peace and in Him we place our faith (like a shield). He is our (helmet of) Salvation and He is the (sword of the Spirit) Word. Jesus is every piece of armor; He is everything we need and His Holy Spirit lives within us. The challenge for us is to utilize the Truth we know in our soul and spirit. When the enemy whispers a frightening possibility to my mind, I have the opportunity to utilize the truth that God has given me peace, and a peace that's not from this world, but a heavenly peace. This peace lives inside of me, but I can also quickly take that situation to the Prince of Peace and trust Him with the battle. Some situations only require the authority given at the mention of His name "Jesus." If you have time, read Ephesians 6:10-19 several times. It's so good. This passage warns us better than any other of the reality of our situation on earth. After describing the armor of God, it goes on to say, *"For our struggle is not against flesh and blood, but against the rulers, against the authorities, against the powers of this dark world and against the spiritual forces of evil in the heavenly realms."*

This is an important truth to understand. We realize from this scripture that the person who hurt you, that thing that was taken from you, or those people who caused you pain are not your enemy. The devil is behind all those experiences; he is the enemy. He uses people just like God uses people. That's the price we pay for having free will I guess. Wouldn't it be great to live in a world where God is the only one with authority to influence people? Someday when we are in heaven, that's what it will be like. But we don't live in heaven, yet. Maybe understanding the fact that people are not our enemy will enable us to begin to love those who have hurt, used and abused us. With the right perspective, we can focus our anger on the true responsible party: the evil forces in high places. Your ex-husband, your boss, your neighbor is not the enemy. If you can picture that hurtful moment in your mind and then picture the devil hovering over and moving through the person who caused you or your loved one pain, it's easier to focus blame on the truly guilty party.

> *"Your ex-husband, your boss, your neighbor is not the enemy."*

Having this perspective frees me from the responsibility that I must somehow bring justice to my situation. I can pray that God will reveal Himself to and bless the lives of my offenders, as Matthew 5:44 instructs. I can ask Jesus to bring them and me to a place of healing and repentance. Only when I can forgive and love, am I truly free. Remember 2 Corinthians 2:10? It speaks of forgiveness. If we can't or won't forgive, the devil has won. He has outwitted us. You may be familiar with the analogy that holding anger and bitterness in your heart is like drinking poison and trying to kill the other person. When we hear that, we know how absurd it is, and yet sometimes we still do it. That bad thinking has fed many cancer cells. It has brought addiction and loneliness to many good people. I'm not saying if you have cancer you need to forgive someone, but … maybe if you have cancer, you do need to forgive someone. {Selah} For me, understanding who the real enemy is enables me to forgive. How else could Jesus have said, as He was dying on the cross, "Father forgive them for they know not what they do." He could show us that example of love and forgiveness because He knew who His true enemy was. Why would God require us to love our enemies and pray for those who persecute us? Because He knows that we are free when we do. He knows that letting go of our need for justice or punishment brings healing, peace and joy.

I probably don't need to say this, but just to be safe, may I add that forgiving doesn't mean we need to stay in an unhealthy place? When I left my church, I had to forgive people that said and did things that wounded me greatly, but God didn't require me to stay. He released me and directed me to where He wanted me to be. We do not need to live as a doormat to honor God. We can say, "No, I'm not going to allow you to continue to…" whatever it is, but then we must let go and trust that God will defend us and make it right in the end. If you're struggling today, know that He's got you. He sees you. He will take care of you.

I have decided that I am completely committed to denying him any influence over me, any thoughts in my mind, any access to my heart, or any more of my time.

TALK TO GOD ABOUT IT

Finally, the last part of Ephesians 6 says in verse 18, *"And pray in the Spirit on all occasions with all kinds of prayers and requests. With this in mind, be alert and always keep on praying for all the saints."* So, once we realize the struggle is spiritual and not of flesh and blood, and after we have begun to utilize the armor given to us in Jesus, we are told to pray. Pray in the Spirit; pray all kinds of prayers; pray for each other; pray and ask for what you desire. Just make sure you pray. May I add to that: pray honest prayers. God knows your heart and He knows your situation. He can take the truth. Many times, I've cried out to God and told Him how angry or sad I was. I never pretend to be anything more than I truly am when I pray. Pray bold prayers. He wants us to ask for and believe for big things, impossible things, miraculous things, because He loves to work miracles in our lives. If you don't know what to pray for in a given situation, pray in the Spirit. Let the Holy Spirit be your guide. When Jesus went away to pray, He went away to be with His Father. Don't let comparison with how others pray intimidate you. You talking with your Father looks and sounds like whatever it looks and sounds like. The important thing is that you pray in faith, placing your trust and expectation in your heavenly Father who created you and loves you more that you can comprehend.

As I wrap up this chapter and reflect on all that I have said, I have come to the realization that I am still living in denial. (And you probably thought that I would tell you that I had figured out how NOT to by now.) But I can't help it; so I've decided since I can't stop, I'll just change the things I'm in denial about. I encourage you to as well. Now my mind is set on denying the devil access to my heart, mind and emotions. He is no longer roaming free in the protection my naivety and denial provided. I am denying him access to the lives of those I love. I am denying him any more territory in my life, and I am reclaiming the territory I have given him in the past. I have decided that I am completely committed to denying him any influence over me, any thoughts in my mind, any access to my heart, or any more of my time. He's done. I can laugh at the days ahead and have peace in the One who has defeated Satan and his demons—the One who holds my days in the palms of His hands and dances over me with singing—Jesus.

Study Guide

What's The Point?

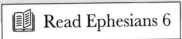

Read Ephesians 6

* What is you main takeaway from this chapter?

* When I think about the devil and what he wants to accomplish in my life, I understand that he wants to make me/keep me ineffective, fearful, confused about who I am and what I have, and he wants me alone and weak.

* The devil knows how powerful we are when we get together and live in unity. He knows the power of forgiveness and the anointing that comes from unity. That is why he does everything he can to pit us against each other—to keep us offended and wounded. We don't have to live that way. We don't have to give him access to our life.

* Take a look at 1 Corinthians 13. When you read it, what stands out with regards to this chapter?

* What does love do? It always…

* I don't know about you, but I don't always do those things. There are times when I just want to give up. There are days when I feel hopeless, and I'm skeptical about people and their motives. It is in those times I am reminded of the Father's love for me and I am motivated to seek Him and receive His amazing love. When I do that, then I can protect, trust, hope and persevere.

* Is there something in your past, a sin you committed, or perhaps a sin that was committed to you, that is keeping you from receiving God's love?

* When you look at other people, does it seem like it is easier for them to know God loves them? Dear one, that's the enemy. He wants to keep you from grasping the Father's great love for you. There is no shame in His love. He is quick to forgive and wash us clean. He forgives our sins as far as the east is from the west. Receive His love for you today.

* Take a moment and talk with God about those experiences and thoughts that are holding you back. Let Him love on you today.

* Think of the relationships and the situations you presently find yourself in. Are there any that could benefit from a little more love?

* Ask God who He wants to pour His love out on today, then give them a call, drop a note in the mail or give them an extra-long hug the next time you see them. Just because.

"We are more than conquerors through Him who loved us. For I am convinced that neither death nor life, neither angels nor demons, neither the present nor the future, nor any powers, neither height nor depth, nor anything else in all creation, will be able to separate us from the love of God that is in Christ Jesus our Lord."
Romans 8:37-39

SUGGESTED READING

The Bondage Breaker
by Neil T. Anderson

9

Confession:
I Don't Want to Die

*"I tell you the truth, unless a kernel of wheat falls to the
ground and dies, it remains only a single seed. But if it
dies, it produces many seeds. The man who loves his life
will lose it, while the man who hates his life in this world
will keep it for eternal life."*
John 12:24

I like to have control. I like to be in control. I don't
like the fact that life is not fair and other people's
choices affect my life. When I find myself in a situation where I am at the mercy of others, which is often, and they are making choices I would definitely not
make, it can be frustrating, to say the least. Consider
road rage and shopping on black Friday, and it's obvious
I'm not alone. We are all presented with choices every

day of how we will respond when life gets stressful. Will we give others the power to steal our peace and our joy? Do we let other people or difficult situations dictate our mood or behavior? I will admit the answer has been "yes" for me much of the time. But, I am learning to see my life and how it relates to others through a different lens. I am allowing the great physician to tweak my perspective yet once again and bring freedom to my soul. I am loosening my grip on everything, learning how to be ok when "it's" not ok and trying not to take things so personally.

CONTROL IS AN ILLUSION

It's not real. What do we really have control of? The definition of the word control means: "The power to influence or direct people's behavior or the course of events. The restriction of an activity, tendency or phenomenon." Or, my favorite, "the power to restrain something, especially one's emotions or actions." If you've ever hit black ice with your car, received a coffee from a drive-thru with the lid almost on, been attracted to someone who was not interested in you, or perhaps planned an outdoor event, you understand how truly powerless we all are. None of us can control another person's response or the wind, rain or heat on the day of that special occasion. We cannot control the unexpected road construction that started two days before our event that slows everything down and makes it difficult to even get to the destination. We can't control the stomach flu that infests the family or the car that pulls out in front of you causing the cake you just picked up to slide on to the floor of your car. You get the point. What can be even more frustrating than all of this is our inability to get other people to do what we want them to, or act like we wish they would. If my husband would only... then I would... if only my child would listen... then I would... if only they would... you fill in the blank.

Through the process of writing this book, I've recently discovered something about myself. As I have asked the Lord to reveal the truth to me and renew my mind and change my thinking, He has mercifully lead me to understand that I have been codependent in many areas of my life. A few months ago, I didn't even know what the term codependent meant. I had heard the term, but I had no idea it could affect so many areas of my life. Then, it was suggested to me by a friend that I attend a codependent workshop. The workshop solidified many of the truths the Lord had been teaching me and working out with me these past few years. It connected all of the dots for me. Many of the revelations I wrote about in this book were codependent tendencies that the Holy Spirit has put His finger on and revealed the truth to me about. I just didn't know there was a term for what I was experiencing. One area where my codependent tendency would manifest was in my need to control. Codependent people often attempt to control someone else's feelings or protect someone from bad feelings, when in reality, none of us have the power over how others think or feel. Codependents also attempt to control the way a person perceives, likes or responds to them. You can see this tendency in the chapter "I'm a People/God Pleaser." Why did I want everyone in my house to be happy all of the time? Why did I try to keep my children from experiencing pain? My motives were out of love, but all I really did was frustrate them and keep them from learning how to deal with the hurt and challenges of this life. I'm sure they learned early on to wear an "I'm fine" mask in an effort not to disappoint me or make me sad, as their sadness or disobedience would sometimes make me sad too. I used to say, "I'm only as happy as my most unhappy child." Codependent. Looking back, I can see how my unrealistic expectations may have caused the people around me to wear a mask pretending everything was alright, when in reality they were hurting. As a result, we didn't deal with the hurt or pain that life brought as much as we could have if everyone were responsible for their own health and happiness. Just so you don't think I'm too hard on myself, I didn't always do this. But any amount was too much and now I'm trying not to live this way at all anymore.

Why did I feel the need to control how others lived their lives? Like somehow, I was responsible for everybody's happiness. Why do I still feel the need sometimes? I've learned to ask the question. I am learning to ask myself when I am getting frustrated by the actions, attitudes or words of others to stop and ask myself why it's affecting me so much. (I'll discuss the main reasons later in this chapter. Hang on; we'll get there.) I can see now that my codependency even bled into my relationship with God. How could it not, when He was such a big part of my life? I can admit that on some level I even tried to control God. I knew that He loved me, that He knew me and had good things for my life, but for some reason, I thought I had to prove to Him how worthy I was of all of that goodness and love. How silly. I now understand I can't manipulate or earn His love no matter how "good" my behavior is. It's about how good He is. It's about relationship. The relationship He initiated when He took my place on the cross and made a way for me to be restored to Him. All I have to do is believe and receive. He's done all of the heavy lifting. I'm currently living from that reality most days, but I still have to remind myself of those truths every once in a while when I start striving to earn what is already mine.

The story of the prodigal (or lost) son as described in Luke 15 is such a great illustration of the Father's heart toward us. It illustrates the point that the Father is more concerned with relationship than He is behavior. It is the perfect example of how controlling God is, or should I say how controlling He is not. The father loves his son enough to give him the freedom to choose. He respected his son enough to make his own decisions, good or bad, and I've learned that respecting others sets me free from my need to control them. My choices say: "I trust you to make your own decisions, and I trust that God will take care of you no matter what." With this understanding, each of us is free to reap the consequences of our own decisions, and as a result, free to love completely. This freedom is not always easy to watch, as I'm sure it was very difficult for God to watch Adam and Eve in the garden. It had to be difficult for the Father (God) in the story of the prodigal son to watch his precious son walk out that door without any remorse or hesitation. But remember, love must have a choice. Without the freedom to choose, we are robots doing as we are told, and that's not love. Without a choice, we can't even obey, because obedience demands a choice as well. God always chooses love. How can He not? He is love. When I read the story of the prodigal son, I relate more to the older brother. I've never been tempted to turn away from the ways of God and live a sinful lifestyle as the prodigal did. However, if you recall, when his brother (the son) returns, the older brother is outraged by the reception he receives from their father. His response demonstrates that he doesn't truly understand the heart of his father. He doesn't realize who he is and what he has. When we act a fool like the prodigal son or his bitter, resentful brother, God is waiting with open arms for us to be restored to Himself—longing for us to understand that we are saved and accepted by grace and not by what we have done.

LET IT GO

In *The Christian Codependence Recovery Workbook*, Stephanie A. Tucker writes:

> *"When we try to control people, we are in fact in direct competition with the Holy Spirit. In 1 Corinthians 2:11, the Bible tells us that no one knows a man but the Spirit that lives in him. As human beings, whenever we take the position of trying to control someone else's thoughts, emotions or behaviors, we are essentially trying to stand in God's shoes. Many times we are unaware how we try to control others and how we have allowed others to control us in relationships. If we are oppressed and dependent on those who control us, it can be extremely challenging and paralyzing. What we must decide is to believe that the power of God truly can overcome those circumstances. We cannot change people, but God can. He can also deliver us from oppression or simply change our own heart so we have the tools and resources to deal with the circumstances appropriately. Normally, as we learn how to cease control in our own relationships, we begin to see that the problems are not just other people but that we in fact have our own dysfunction. God will reveal to us our faulty beliefs and the negative systems we use to make relationships work.*
>
> *Letting go comes with a realization that we will be empty-handed, at least for a period. In the long term, the idea of a healthy form of letting go is that there is something better to cling to. It's a realization that whatever we are holding on to doesn't really belong to us, and we need to be willing to set it free from our grip."* [8]

Thank you, Stephanie, for your words of wisdom!

I have learned, other people's choices are not my responsibility just because I love them, and I cannot control how someone else feels or reacts.

Sometimes we think we are Holy Spirit Jr. and if we don't intervene, a catastrophe will happen. The problem is, it might. That person might leave. He might take another drink. She might choose friends that will inevitably take her down a destructive and possibly dangerous path. But it's his choice. It's her path to choose. The question I need to ask myself is, "Is it my responsibility? Is it my problem?" I've often thought it was. As a mother, a wife and even a faithful friend, I've confused empathy with responsibility. In times when I should have felt compassion and a prompting to

> *"But I have learned, other people's choices are not my responsibility just because I love them, and I cannot control how someone else feels or reacts."*

pray, I took on some of the responsibility to keep the peace, to meet the need and bring truth or judgment to the situation. But I have learned, other people's choices are not my responsibility just because I love them, and I cannot control how someone else feels or reacts. In those times, my responsibility is to pray, to speak the truth in love and let go. Ahh! I wish that were easier for me.

Having said all of that, I'm reminded of what it says in Galatians 5:22, *"But the fruit of the Spirit is love, joy, peace, patience, kindness, goodness, faithfulness, gentleness, and self-control."* Ahh, so I do have control! I can control myself. I can control, with the help of the Holy Spirit, my tongue, my attitude, my choices and even my mood. I am not helpless when it comes to my flesh. The same Spirit that raised Christ from the dead lives in me.

WORRY ABOUT YOURSELF

There is a video that has been going around for some time now of a little girl named Rose; she's maybe two years old. She is trying to fasten her seatbelt by herself, and she tells her father, rather forcefully, to "worry about yourself." Her father asks if she needs help, and with her precious little voice she says, "No, no tank you. You drive. Worry about yourself." (Go to YouTube and check it out.) It's funny because obviously, she needs help, but I love her tenacious spirit. She does make the point: if we would all just "take care of ourselves" life would be more peaceful and more enjoyable. Rose is obviously not codependent. I hope she can keep it that way.

Think about a relationship in your life that is stressed, or even worse, filled with anger and resentment. Now imagine if each of you spent time with the true source of life independently, enabling each of you to concern yourself only with your own feelings and actions. (I can hear Louis Armstrong singing

What a Wonderful World now.) What if when that person was immature or selfish or mean, you decided by the overflow of the Spirit of God that is within you to manage the only thing you can manage: your own response. How great would it be if each of you were full of the Spirit of self-control empowering you to be quick to listen, slow to speak and slow to become angry? Then each of you could "worry about yourself" and not need to be right the next time there was a confrontation. Imagine what that would look like. It would look like heaven.

I guess I do have some control, self-control. How do I become more self-controlled, even more fruitful? In John 15:5, Jesus says, *"I am the vine; you are the branches. If a man remains in me and I in him, he will bear much fruit; apart from me you can do nothing."* So, if I remain in Him, I will be fruitful. Seems too easy. It just might be. When I looked up a synonym for the word remain, the first word that was listed was rest. To rest in Him, and I would add, to trust in Him, seems so simple, but simple does not necessarily mean easy. Selah.

I've heard it said that time equals power. I guess this concept of remaining is what they are talking about. Time spent in the secret place of His presence. Time spent trusting God and loving others. The more I connect to The Source, the more I place my hope and trust in Him, the easier it will be for me to control myself, to have an abundance of joy and peace, and to love people like Jesus. I can't become more fruitful on my own. I can't do anything of value for the

Kingdom on my own. I've tried. It didn't work. My will power is not self-control. When I pull up my boot straps and try really hard, it works for a while, until it doesn't anymore. That's when I blow it, or I blow up. I can't manage it on my own. If I am going to live with any kind of consistency, I must be empowered by the Holy Spirit. The ability to authentically live with more love, joy, peace, patience, kindness, goodness, gentleness, faithfulness, and self-control must be a fruit of God's Spirit, a byproduct of my source, the Lord.

I get to choose my source. I get to choose it every day. That is another thing I have control over. The Bible tells us in Deuteronomy to "choose life." Choosing life means choosing the Kingdom, choosing God's ways over the world's ways. It means I choose to believe the Word of God is true, and even though I don't understand all of it fully, I place myself under its authority and seek to let The Truth bring wisdom and revelation to my spirit and soul (my mind, will and emotions). I recognize that left to myself I will choose myself or this world every time.

This brings me back to John 12:24-25 mentioned at the beginning of the chapter: *"I tell you the truth, unless a kernel of wheat falls to the ground and dies, it remains only a single seed. But if it dies, it produces many seeds. The man who loves his life will lose it, while the man who hates his life in this world will keep it for eternal life."*

But if it dies, it produces many seeds. Hmm. Death to self brings abundant life to me and to those around me. But I don't want to die! Left to myself, I want to protect what is mine. I want to defend myself and promote myself. After all, isn't that human nature? Yes, it is. As long as we are living from a place of fear and insecurity, we will always need to protect, defend, guard, etc. You may be thinking to yourself, What fear? What are you afraid of? Rejection. Being unloved or unwanted. Failure, just to name a few. These are not things I consciously think about, but when I am feeling insecure or angry or feeling the need to control, I have learned to ask myself: What's the root? Why do I feel the need to protect myself from people? Why am I afraid to take a risk and try that new thing? That's when I remind myself of who I am and whose I am. I remind myself that God calls me his daughter, His beloved one. I place my faith in what He's told me to do, and what His Word tells me about who He is and who I am. He is my defender and the lover of my soul. If I trust in Him and place my life in His hands again, He will never leave me or forsake me. He's good. His plans for me are good and He loves me. People can do whatever they will do. I don't need to control or manipulate them, and I don't need to be afraid. Living in fear and insecurity is our old nature. "We are new creations in Christ" as described in 2 Corinthians 5. We no longer live for ourselves. We received a new nature when we gave our lives to Christ. We call Him Lord because we trust Him, and that's how we can yield to His will, His Word, and to His authority. Jesus said it this way in Luke 9:23-24, *"If anyone wishes to come after Me, he must deny himself, and take up his cross daily and follow Me. For whoever wishes to save his life will lose it, but whoever loses his life for My sake, he is the one who will save it."* I like how Paul put it when he was inspired by the Holy Spirit to write to the Galatians. He said in Galatians 5:24, *"Now those who belong to Christ Jesus have crucified the flesh with its passions and desires."*

The process of yielding is just that—a process. As Christ is revealed to us, we begin to trust Him. Here we are again, back to trust. As we know Him more and begin to trust Him more, we find it easier to yield, or I could say to surrender to Him. As the car that is already rolling is easier to steer, so is a surrendered heart willing to surrender again and again. Maybe it's time to put your car in D and give it a little gas. The process of bowing our knee and giving everything to Jesus can be scary, but that's only because it's new. Once you've learned that you can trust Him and that He really is good, it gets easier, until one day you find yourself bowing to His will and yielding to His Spirit without hesitation.

Surrender is a journey. The process of sanctification will continue until the day we die and see Jesus face to face. So we're not perfect. That's ok. That's why we need grace. God's grace is abundant, dare I say amazing. Paul said it this way in 2 Corinthians 12:8-9, *"But he said to me, 'My grace is sufficient for you, for my power is made perfect in weakness.' Therefore I will boast all the more gladly about my weaknesses, so that Christ's power may rest on me.* "We're not going to get it right all of the time. But if we are living surrendered to Christ and trusting in His will for our lives, He will be glorified, and isn't that the goal after all?!

If you have never fully surrendered your heart and your life to Christ, may I encourage you to take that next step? Perhaps you have surrendered your life, but you are still protecting that one hurt you don't talk about to anyone from Him. He is gentle and kind and waiting to take your life in His hands and bring salvation, restoration and healing to every area of your life. Take a moment now and talk to Jesus. Lay it down. Surrender to Jesus. It's time. What are you afraid of?

GOODBYE FOR NOW

As I complete this chapter, I am grateful for all that God has done in my life through the process of writing this book. He is magnificent! Writing these concepts and confessions has been an absolute labor of love for me. As I have sat down to write, asking the Lord to use me and speak through me, I have seen your face and grown to love your heart. I've seen you on the street, in the coffee shop and next to me at church, and He has endeared you to me. He has poured out His love on us and we can't go back. I'm so glad. Thank you for reading to the end and being open to what God is saying. I pray that you have found a level of truth and freedom you did not possess when you selected this book with its curious title. Please test everything you have read against scripture, as I am far from perfect and still on a journey of revelation and truth. Hopefully, some of the perspectives shared in these pages have initiated conversations with others that will provoke study and motivate you to find the answers for yourself with the Holy Spirit as your guide. I hope that you have been challenged in your thinking, set free in some of the areas that were holding you back and encountered the Lord in a greater way. It is my prayer that you feel lighter and a little less encumbered by the weight of doing better and being better for Jesus—that the gospel you know and share is more about relationship than behavior. It is my prayer that the Holy Physician has tweaked your perspective and brought His love, His grace and His mercy into greater focus in your life.

It's so easy to be earthly-minded, only pursuing and responding to what we can see, feel and hear, but if we will make ourselves available to what our Heavenly Father is saying to us and doing in the earth, we can partner with Him. What a privilege; what a joy!

"It's so easy to be earthly-minded, only pursuing and responding to what we can see, feel and hear, but if we will make ourselves available to what our Heavenly Father is saying to us and doing in the earth, we can partner with Him. What a privilege; what a joy!"

Matthew 6:9 says, *"Thy kingdom come, thy will be done, on earth as it is in heaven."* God is changing my mindset. I hope

through the process of reading this book, He is changing yours as well. It's so easy to be earthly-minded, only pursuing and responding to what we can see, feel and hear, but if we will make ourselves available to what our Heavenly Father is saying to us and doing in the earth, we can partner with Him. What a privilege; what a joy! His Word brings life and His ways are true. He has amazing plans for your life. Trust Him. When you find yourself doing things to please God, pause and remember that if you trust Him in all things, He will be pleased.

As I say goodbye, may I encourage you to slow down and let the Father love you. He's wanting to reveal Himself to you and pour out His great love on you. He's waiting in the sunset, in the hug of a friend or in anything that draws your heart toward Him. When you are down or feel afraid, wondering how you will make it through, fix your eyes on Jesus dear sister. When you seek Him, you will find Him. He is always an ever-present help in time of need. I need Him every day. Don't you?

"Seek first the kingdom and His righteousness, and all these things will be added to you as well. Therefore do not worry about tomorrow, for tomorrow will worry about itself." Matthew 6:33

What's The Point?

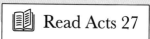 Read Acts 27

* What is your main takeaway from this chapter?

* Acts 27 tells the story of Paul, a prisoner, on a ship with men that wouldn't listen to him, in weather he couldn't control. He had control over nothing, except his attitude and response. He remained positive and faithful, and if you read on to chapter 28, you'll see that the miraculous power of Christ was on display in his life. Well, I guess that's how you do it right there. We should follow Paul's example as he follows Christs.

* In what area of your life do you struggle the most with regards to not having control? Family, work, politics, etc.

* Who in your life are you trying to control? I can think of a few people. But then I remind myself of how disrespectful it is to them and to God. I remind myself to "worry about myself," and it brings me peace.

* Does reading this chapter inspire you to "let go and let God"? If so, what does that look like, practically speaking?

* Surrendering your life to Christ is the best decision you will ever make. To me, living a life where you are the one in charge, telling God what you want Him to do for you, is like driving with the parking brake on. You can move forward, but it's rough; there is resistance, and it's noisy. When you surrender control of your life to Jesus, the brake is released and the ride is smoother, quieter and way more peaceful. With the parking brake on, the engine will eventually fail. When it is released, the car will drive for miles and miles.

* Surrender is a process. We yield, and then when life happens, we yield some more. Are you willing to surrender your life (again) to Jesus? Are you ready to let Him take the place of Lord in your life?

* If you're hesitating or your answer is "no," maybe it's because you don't trust that He will do what is really best for you. Maybe you need to ask Him to reveal Himself to you in a greater way. He will, you know. He promises: "When you seek me, you will find me."

* If Jesus had to surrender to the will of His Father, how much more should we?

* What are some scriptures that reveal Jesus yielding to the will of Father God?

"For it is with your heart that you believe and are justified, and it is with your mouth that you confess and are saved. As the Scripture says, 'Anyone who trusts in Him will never be put to shame.'" Romans 10:10-11

SUGGESTED READING

———

The Christian Codependence Recovery Workbook by Stephanie A. Tucker

NOTES

1. Dayna Drum, "It's Time to Address Spiritual Abuse in the Church," RelevantMagazine.com, October 27, 2014

2. "#158: Healing from Spiritual Abuse: Part 2." YouTube video, 49:48. Posted by "Mark DeJesus," July 5, 2017. https://www.youtube.com/watch?v=SinVqkaV4Pc&t=2s

3. Lynch, John, Bruce McNicol, and Bill Thrall. The Cure: What if God isn't who you think He is and neither are you. 2011. 3rd ed. San Clemente: CrossSection, 2016, 20.

4. Lynch, McNicol, Thrall. The Cure. 30.

5. Davis, G. Holy Ground. Meadowgreen Music Company/ Songchannel Music Co, 1983.

6. Houston, J., Crocker, M., Ligthelm, S., Oceans. Hillsong Music Publishing, 2012.

7. Anderson, Neil. Victory Over the Darkness. 2000. Bloomington: Bethany House Publishers, 2013, 128.

8. Tucker, Stephanie A. The Christian Codependence Recovery Workbook: From Surviving to Significance. Huntington Beach: Spirit of Life Recovery, 2010, 112-113.